Authors

1. Alecia Francois (Learning 2 Walk)
2. Alida Quittschreiber (The Realistic Mama)
3. Amanda Boyarshinov (The Educators' Spin On It)
4. Amanda Vasquez (Artsy Momma)
5. Amy Pessolano (Umbrella Tree Cafe)
6. Amy Powell (Learning and Exploring Through Play)
7. Amy Smith, M.Ed. (Wildflower Ramblings)
8. Ana Taney (Mommy's Bundle)
9. Angela Thayer (Teaching Mama)
10. Anne Carey (Left Brain Craft Brain)
11. Aysh Siddiqua (Words n Needles)
12. Becca Eby (Bare Feet on the Dashboard)
13. Becky Mansfield (Your Modern Family)
14. Becky Moseley (Tales of Beauty for Ashes)
15. Birute Efe (Playtivities)
16. Brittany Morazan (Love, Play, Learn)
17. Caitlyn "Suzy" Stock (Suzy Homeschooler)
18. Candace Lindemann (Naturally Educational)
19. Carly Seifert (Africa to America)
20. Christie Burnett (Childhood 101)
21. Christie Kiley (Mama OT)
22. Christina Schul (There's Just One Mommy)
23. Cindy Ingram (The Art Curator for Kids)
24. Colleen Beck, OTR/L (Mommy Needs a Coffee Break & Sugar Aunts)
25. Crystal Chatterton (The Science Kiddo)
26. Crystal McClean (Castle View Academy)
27. Danielle Buckley (Mom Inspired Life)
28. Danya (Danya Banya)
29. Dayna Abraham (Lemon Lime Adventures)
30. Deb Chitwood, M.A. (Living Montessori Now)
31. Deborah (Mommy Crusader and her Knights and Ladies)
32. Denise Bertacchi (stlMotherhood)
33. Dhiyana (Edutainment At Home)
34. Ellen (Cutting Tiny Bites)
35. Emma Edwards (Adventures of Adam)
36. Erica (What Do We Do All Day?)
37. Erica Leggiero (eLeMeNOP Kids)
38. Erica Loop (Mini Monets and Mommies)
39. Georgina Bomer (Craftulate)
40. Gude (Hodge Podge Craft)
41. Heather Greutman (Golden Reflections Blog)
42. Helen Newberry(Peakle Pie & Witty Hoots)
43. Holly Homer (Kids Activities Blog)
44. Rachel Miller (Kids Activities Blog)
45. Jackie Houston (I Heart Arts n Crafts)
46. Jacquie Fisher (Edventures with Kids)
47. Jaime Williams (Frogs and Snails and Puppy Dog Tail)
48. Jamie Hand (Hand Made Kids Art)
49. Jamie Reimer (hands on : as we grow)
50. Jennifer Tammy (Study at Home Mama)
51. Jill Morgenstern (Do Try This at Home)
52. Jodie Rodriguez (Growing Book by Book)
53. Julie Kirkwood (Creekside Learning)
54. Julie Nixon (My Mundane and Miraculous Life)
55. Kara Carrero (ALLterNATIVElearning)
56. Katie Pinch (A Little Pinch of Perfect)
57. Katie S-G (Gift of Curiosity)
58. Katie T. Christiansen (Preschool Inspirations)
59. Kristina Buskirk (Toddler Approved)
60. Kristina Couturier (School Time Snippets)
61. Laura Marschel (Lalymom)
62. Laura R (Sunny Day Family)
63. Liska Myers (Adventure in a Box)
64. Louise McMullen (Messy Little Monster)
65. Maggy Woodley (Red Ted Art)
66. Mama Carmody (Love to Laugh and Learn)
67. Marie Mack (Child Led Life)
68. MaryAnne (Mama Smiles)
69. Melissa Lennig (Fireflies and Mud Pies)
70. Menucha (Moms & Crafters)
71. Mihaela Vrban (Best Toys 4 Toddlers)
72. Monique Boutsiv (Living Life and Learning)
73. Mummy Kettle (101 things to do with kids)
74. Nadia (Teach me Mommy)
75. Nicola Simpson (Crafty Kids at Home)
76. Nicolette Roux (Powerful Mothering)
77. Rachel Coley (CanDo Kiddo)
78. Rebecca Reid (Line upon Line Learning)
79. Sarah E. White (Our Daily Craft)
80. Sarah Punkoney, MAT (Stay At Home Educator)
81. Sharla Orren (Look At What You Are Seeing)
82. Sheila Rogers (Brain Power Boy)
83. Shelah (Mosswood Connections)
84. Sheryl Cooper (Teaching 2 and 3 Year Olds)
85. Shruti (Artsy Craftsy Mom)
86. Sue Lively (One Time Through)
87. Suzanne Schlechte (My Buddies and I)
88. Tammy (Housing A Forest)
89. Terri Thompson (Creative Family Fun)
90. Theresa (Capri + 3)
91. Tonya Cooley (Therapy Fun Zone)
92. Vanessa (Mama's Happy Hive)
93. Victoria Armijo (ABC Creative Learning)
94. Victoria Milne McInnes (Squiggles and Bubbles)

kid blogger network

Spelling and Grammar

This book is a contribution of 94 authors from all over the world. Each author has used their own style of writing, spelling and grammar for their respective areas. Words such as color /colour and center /centre will be found in the activities below.

Due to the large collaborative nature, this book is a self-published work. This means that despite having many eyes on the final edits and proof reads, it is not perfect and may contain some grammatical errors. Our aim is to bring you wonderful things to do and teach your child through play.

Many of our authors are teachers, occupational therapists, experienced homeschoolers and hands on moms. Some even hold degrees in other fields!

. . . .

A Note About Safety

The activities in this book are intended to be done under adult supervision. Appropriate and reasonable caution is required at all times. Beware when using small materials and tools suggested in this book, including but not limited to scissors, hot glue or objects that could pose a choking hazard. Observe safety and caution at all times.

The authors of this book disclaim all liability for any damage, mishap or injury that may occur from engaging in activities in this book.

. . . .

Copyright

First Edition | 2015
Kid Blogger Network | http://kidbloggernetwork.com

Foreword

Welcome, from all the members of the Kid Blogger Network!

I'm Jamie, the creator and founder behind the Kid Blogger Network (KBN). I created KBN as a place to brainstorm and collaborate with like-minded bloggers. The KBN became a place for friends, peers and colleagues to bring the best out in each other for you, our reader, other parents, teachers and caregivers.

The talented members of the KBN have taken many projects into their own hands to create something amazing. This book is one of those projects. Members have collaborated together to create an amazing resource for caregivers of all sorts. Whether you're looking for a rainy day activity at home, an activity for homeschooling or for in the classroom, this KBN book is a collection of the best mom (& teacher) tested activities and ideas! Have fun!

Jamie Reimer
www.handsonaswegrow.com

. . . .

How to Use This Book

Activity Name

abilities targeted

Circles indicate age suggestions and if a printable is available at the back of the book.

Printables are also available for download: https://goo.gl/tImjEH

items required for activity

how to

Author Name - Blog Name

About the author and blog url

Table of Contents

Table of Contents continued

"You can discover more about a person in an hour of play than in a year of conversation."

- Plato

General Play

Art & Crafts

Activities

Science Challenge: Rock Collection

Math, Counting, Size Sorting, Science, Science Experiments, Writing

Toddler

Pre-school

Kinder-garten

You will need:

Assortment of rocks
Magnifying glass
Paper
Pencil or marker

How to:

I challenge parents and caregivers to integrate more science into your child's everyday activities. This particular activity requires very little preparation and the materials you need are right outside your door - ROCKS. A magnifying glass is a great addition this activity, but not a necessity. Set aside 30 minutes this week to find, compare and discuss the rock collection with your child.

Learning Objective: Observe and describe similarities and differences in rocks.

Directions for the Rock Collection Activity
1. The child will collect rocks on their daily adventures outdoors. Tell him that a rock is a natural solid made up of one or more minerals.

2. Once a group of five or more rocks have been collected, encourage him to observe the shape, textures, weight and colors of each rock. Talk about what he sees. Use language-rich words such as shiny, dull, smooth, bumpy, round, flat, heavy, light, and hard.

3. Allow the child to organize his collection in any way he chooses. Encourage him to then sort by certain attributes as described earlier. Find a place in the home or classroom where this collection can be displayed.

4. After the collection has been sorted, choose one rock to draw in a science journal. Label colors, divots, textures, or differences in the rock that makes it unique. Write one sentence to describe the attributes of that particular rock. Preschool children may attempt to write these words on their own. An adult may also write the words dictated by the child in grown-up writing on the paper. This helps beginning writers make the connection between spoken words and written words.

Amanda Boyarshinov - The Educators' Spin On It

THE EDUCATORS' SPIN ON IT
Amanda Boyarshinov is a master teacher and one of the bloggers behind the parenting and education site The Educators' Spin On It. She shares her teaching knowledge with parents everywhere through her creative, inventive writing including her latest e-book, STEAM, STEM Enrichment Activities for Preschoolers E-Book. http://www.theeducatorsspinonit.com/

Tissue Paper and Water Art

Color Learning

Toddler

Pre-school

You will need:

Tissue paper in different colors
Scissors
White cardstock
Water
Paintbrush

How to:

Using tissue paper and water is a really fun way to create artwork and is suitable for a wide range of ages!

In advance of the activity, prepare lots of tissue paper pieces by cutting them up into different shapes. Older children can help tear or cut up the paper.

Provide a brush, a little water, some white card and the tissue paper pieces. Show your child how to stick the tissue paper to the card by brushing some water lightly over the top.

Try not to let your child spread too much water as the card will get too soggy! If you think this is likely to happen you may want to ensure that you do this activity with something protecting your surface as some of the dye from the tissue paper may leak through the card.

Leave the artwork to dry overnight. The next day the tissue paper pieces will be starting to peel off – kids can help remove them! The pieces leave the dye on the card, creating some unusual artwork. It looks rather like a stained glass window!

After the card is completely dry, you can either enjoy the artwork as it is or perhaps make it into something else. It can be folded and used as a greeting card, or as a fun background for another craft! Note – the tissue paper bundle that I used included some metallic gold and silver paper. The color didn't run from these pieces at all!

Seasonal variations:
Red and pink tissue paper for Valentine's Day
Pastel tissue paper for Easter
Red and green tissue paper for Christmas

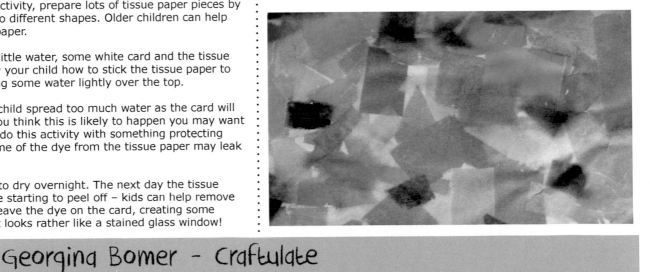

Georgina Bomer - Craftulate

Craftulate
Making Learning Fun.

Georgina writes the blog Craftulate, which features art, craft and activities for young children. She enjoys working her son's interests into their activities to help him learn and develop. She is the author of Art, Craft & Cooking with Toddlers and 50 Animal Crafts for Little Kids. http://www.craftulate.com/

Calm Down Sensory Bottle

Sensory, Science

- Baby
- Toddler
- Pre-school
- Kinder garten

You will need:

Empty and clean water bottle
Hot water
Clear tacky glue
Liquid watercolor or food coloring
Fine glitter
Hot glue or super glue
Mixing bowl
Whisk

How to:

Calm down discovery bottles are wonderful and mesmerizing sensory bottles that swirl glitter around for several minutes. They are absolutely captivating and great for relaxing, calming down a mildly upset child, and just enjoying. I think they are perfect for adults as well!

We use them in our library area and quiet areas as well as for props in the kids' play kitchen. Sometimes when I have a child who is having trouble calming down, I will offer them the calm down jar. They are already familiar with it by this point which assures me that the child will use it appropriately instead of using it for destructive purposes.

Here's how I made this one, which suspends the glitter in beautiful swirls for about three minutes.

You will be filling your empty water bottle according to proportions of tacky glue to water. I recommend filling the bottle with 1/4 clear tacky glue and 3/4 water. Make sure to leave some space at the top in case you want to add more glue or water.

Detailed instructions:
Pour clear tacky glue and hot water into the mixing bowl, along with some liquid watercolor or food coloring, and glitter. Add as much food coloring and glitter as desired. Now mix with the whisk. When everything is blended, mix vigorously then pour right away into the water bottle. The last stir helps get the glitter to transfer to the water bottle instead of settling in the mixing bowl. I just add a bit more hot water to the mixing bowl if there is some that is stuck. Then I clean the residual glitter out with a paper towel before rinsing and cleaning it out.

Feel free to put the lid on and shake to make sure your calm down jar is working its magic. If you want the glitter to suspend longer, add more tacky glue. If you would like it to fall more quickly, add water. Then I leave the lid off until the water lowers to room temperature. After your bottle is just the way you like it, let it cool without the lid. Once it has cooled, I put the lid back on and secure it with hot glue or super glue.

Now you have hours of glittery entertainment and relaxation that your child can easily carry around.

Katie T. Christiansen - Preschool Inspirations

Katie has worked as an early childhood professional for over 13 years and has a degree in Early Childhood Education. She has enjoyed working as both a teacher and preschool administrator and currently does both as she owns and operates her own private preschool out of her home while homeschooling her two children at the same time. Her passion lies in play-based learning, and she loves sharing her knowledge, activities, and adventures. http://preschoolinspirations.com/

Homemade Play Dough

Fine Motor, Sensory, Play Recipes

Baby

Toddler

Pre-
school

Kinder-
garten

You will need:

1/2 cup All Purpose flour
1/2 cup water
2 Tbsp salt
1 teaspoon cream of tartar
2-3 drops food dye

How to:

This recipe for homemade play dough makes a fairly small batch of dough, so you may want to make a few batches in different colors.

In a saucepan (preferably nonstick), mix the first four ingredients together so the mixture is as smooth as possible. It is OK if a few little lumps remain. Add the food dye and stir to mix thoroughly. Add more dye if required.

Heat slowly, stirring regularly. As the mixture starts to thicken, stir constantly. Soon it will begin to pull away from the sides of the saucepan and form one lump. This takes about five minutes.

Remove from the heat and place the play dough ball on some parchment paper. Let it cool slightly and then knead it for a minute or so.

If you want to make several colors it is best to do the heating and stirring part one color at a time – as each dough needs your full attention once you start cooking!

The play dough can be stored by wrapping it in parchment paper and placing it in a resealable zipper bag.

Note: This dough could be eaten, although it doesn't taste that nice so I wouldn't recommend it! But if your child likes to experiment by putting everything in their mouth – this dough would at least be taste-safe for them.

Why not try some variations to your play dough? You could add in some glitter, scented oils or extracts for an increased sensory experience.

Georgina Bomer - Craftulate

Georgina writes the blog Craftulate, which features art, craft and activities for young children. She enjoys working her son's interests into their activities to help him learn and develop. She is the author of Art, Craft & Cooking with Toddlers and 50 Animal Crafts for Little Kids. http://www.craftulate.com/

Craftulate
Making. Learning. Fun.

Velcro Grabbing Wall

Milestone Encouragement, Fine Motor, DIY Toys, Shapes, Literacy, Reading, ABC

Baby

Toddler

Pre-school

You will need:

Laminator or self-laminating sheets (I prefer Scotch brand self-sealing pouches)
Scissors
Self-adhesive Velcro strips
Images: family photographs, magazine clippings, black and white images, copied images from children's books
Baby-safe manipulatives and toys

How to:

With low-cost supplies and simple set-up, a Velcro grabbing wall makes a fun playroom or nursery addition that will grow with your child for years to come.

To make your Velcro grabbing wall:
Adhere the scratchy side of a 12 – 18 inch strip of self-adhesive Velcro onto a clean section of wall or baseboard. The ideal height will vary based on the age of your child – 6-12 inch high for babies under 1 and 12-24 inch high for toddlers and preschoolers.

Use your scissors to cut small squares of the soft side of Velcro. Rounding the corners as you cut will help the Velcro stick better and using the soft side will make baby less interested in scratching at and peeling the Velcro off of objects that they grab. Adhere the small squares of Velcro to laminated images or baby-safe toys. The sky is the limit with what you can put on your Velcro grabbing wall, but here are some ideas for different age groups:

Newborns won't be ready for grabbing but can enjoy visually exploring items on the Grabbing Wall in Tummy Time, while lying on their side or while belly-up to promote head turning.
-laminated black and white pictures
-photographs of the faces of family members

Bigger babies will enjoy items on the grabbing wall that they can grasp, pull down, tap together, look at and put in containers. You can also use images and objects related to children's books and songs.
-blocks
-laminated seasonal images from magazines
-stacking cups
-laminated images from children's books (reduce the size when copying, if necessary)
-laminated animal photos or animal toys for singing "Old MacDonald" and other animal songs

Toddlers & Preschoolers will stay busy grabbing, building and placing items on the wall in pretend play. You can also include materials for early literacy such as matching, rhyming and reading.
-shapes from a shape sorter toy
-puzzle pieces
-toy cars or trains
-play food
-laminated pairs of shapes, pictures or paint chips for matching
-plastic or foam letters and numbers

**Close supervision (eyes on child within arm's reach) is required due to the fact that velcro can become a choking hazard if removed from objects.

Rachel Coley - CanDo Kiddo

Rachel Coley, MS, OTR/L, has been a pediatric Occupational Therapist for 8 years. Rachel blogs about creative play for babies' healthy development. http://www.candokiddo.com/

Dinosaur Fossil Excavation

Fine Motor, Sensory, Imagination Play, Science, Science Experiments

Toddler

Pre-school

Kinder-garten

You will need:

Dinosaur fossils
Edible dirt, which consists of a box of chocolate cake mix, crushed Oreos, and whole-wheat flour
Shallow plastic bin
Brush (You can use an old makeup brush or they can be found at the dollar store)
Plastic shovel
Rocks (optional)

How to:

Do you have a dinosaur fanatic? I think almost every kid goes through a dinosaur phase. This is a fun, educational sensory experience that is great for your dinosaur kid! This activity is good for kids of all ages and is safe for toddlers who put everything in their mouths since the dirt is edible!

This activity provides exploration using all 5 senses. It teaches observation and other scientific principles as well as providing teaching opportunities for learning about fossils, excavation, and dinosaurs.

Step 1- Arrange your fossils in the bottom of your bin.

Step 2- Fill your bin with your edible dirt. You can add each ingredient separately or mix them all together. Putting one on the left side, one in the center, and one on the right is great because of the different texture each of the dirt ingredients provides. The dirt looks realistic after they are combined after

the excavation begins.

Step 3- Add your rocks (I washed them before adding) and any other props you may want to add.

Step 4- Begin your excavation! Let your little Paleontologist dig and/or use the brush to find the dinosaur fossils.

Step 5- Use it as a learning opportunity and vocabulary builder by talking about the meaning of observation, excavation, fossils, and dinosaurs. Every time you find a fossil, talk about which dinosaur the fossil belongs to.

This is a must do activity for any dinosaur lover! It is fun and educational and you never have to worry about young children putting it in their mouth! When your child is done playing with it, you can put the lid on the bin and store it away for later use. They are going to want to play with it over and over!

TIP: Use a "mess mat" for easy cleanup. I just use a plastic shower curtain liner. This would also be a great outdoor activity.

Brittany Morazan - Love, Play, Learn

Brittany Morazan is a mom to two beautiful little hooligans. She blogs about kids activities and crafts, parenting and family at Love, Play, Learn. http://loveplayandlearn.com/

I've Got Rhythm!

Gross Motor, Imagination Play

Toddler

Pre-school

Kinder-garten

You will need:

Teddy bear or other stuffed animal
Music that your child enjoys
Movement scarves or other props suitable for dancing

How to:

I firmly believe that all children are born musical. Even though your child may not grow up to become the next Beethoven or Bach, he can be taught music appreciation and basic musical skills at an early age.

Why teach rhythm and tempo to little ones?
Rhythm and tempo are musical concepts that can be taught playfully; understanding them will help deepen your child's appreciation of music. Should your child go on to take formal lessons, the rhythmic experiences you gave him as a tot will help him to count well and express himself musically more naturally and easily.

Teddy Bear Rhythms:
This chant and activity pre-teaches rhythm notations. Grab a teddy bear or other favorite stuffed animal and bounce it up and down to the beat indicated in the parentheses. Repeat each chant several times.

(Quarter note rhythm)
Teddy Bear, Teddy Bear, march march march march
(Half note rhythm)
Teddy Bear, Teddy Bear, stand-ing stand-ing

(Eighth note rhythm)
Teddy Bear, Teddy Bear, runn-ing runn-ing runn-ing runn-ing
(Whole note rhythm)
Teddy Bear, Teddy Bear, sleeeeeeeep (stretch out sleep for 4 beats – a whole note)

You can also try marching to these chants with your child, or playing a rhythm instrument — such as a drum or tambourine – as you chant.

Scarf Dancing
Rhythm activities should always include movement of some sort! Turn on some music for your child to enjoy and give him some movement scarves or other props to move with. Though the temptation may be to always crank up the nursery rhymes or Raffi, I would also encourage you to explore exciting classical or multicultural tunes, such as Carnival of the Animals or African-style rhythm songs.

Begin by calling out a speed that your child should move to – fast, slow, walking-speed, running speed. You may also wish to use the fancy Italian music terminology – vivace (fast and lively), allegro (fast), andante (walking speed) and largo (slowly).

Name emotions for him to express through his movements – sad, tired, shy, excited, and afraid. This helps him understand that music is a way to express emotions as he feels the connection between music and his body.

Tip: Participate in the music-making with your child! If your child is inhibited, seeing you move around and be silly will help him relax. Music-making is more successful and enjoyable when it is a family experience!

Carly Seifert - Africa to America

Carly is the mom of two little ones, and teaches piano and writing classes. She is passionate about raising global citizens, and blogs about adoption and parenting, while also sharing loads of multicultural reads and learning activities. http://www.africatoamerica.org/

Thrift Shop Busy Bags

DIY Toys, Busy Bags

Baby

Toddler

Pre-school

Kinder-garten

You will need:

A thrifty shopping trip

How to:

Thrift shop finds can sometimes be the most exciting purchases because who doesn't love finding something that should cost them $50 for just a couple of bucks?! My love of thrift shops made me want to figure out how to make busy bags from neglected, but awesome thrift finds.

Rules for Making Busy Bags
While you do not have to follow these rules, here are some rules I have made for our busy bags that I sometimes break.
1. Aim for six items or less in each busy bag.
2. Try to go for easily replaceable or make it something you're not afraid to lose.
3. Make sure your bags teach something.
4. Stick to a single concept or theme.
5. Make them fun.

Get Some Bags!
I love going into thrift stores and looking at their selection and variety of bags. There are so many in every thrift store and most of the time you can get the bags for $1 or less. This allows you to get a variety of shapes, sizes and colors. I like not having any two bags the same because I know what is in each of them.

We love finding great toys in thrift stores that have pieces

missing. In fact, we continually come up with ways to utilize stray toys. There is no reason that an awesome puzzle has to be at the end of its life just because it has a piece or two missing. Just put them in a bag with some note cards and a crayon to make great tracing games or a simple travel matching game. Plus, look for other "puzzle-like" games which have lots of pieces that can be used in new ways.

Look For Toys That Are Only A Partial Set
I not only find puzzles without pieces or pieces without their puzzle, I also find a lot of toys that are not with their complete set. From magnetic dolls and their clothes to Magnatiles and pretend tools, I have been able to collect some great toys to put in busy bags to make a fun, new educational activity. We have also put together bags with little people and characters that don't have all of the people there and other ideas.

Kara Carrero - ALLterNATIVElearning

Kara is a former classroom teacher turned homeschooler, curriculum writer, and web consultant. Her passion has always been in education in whatever form that takes. She blogs at ALLterNATIVElearning about natural parenting, tot school, and living sustainably. http://ALLterNATIVElearning.com/

15

Leaf Art Activity

Fine Motor, Imagination Play, Shapes, Size Sorting

Toddler

Pre-school

Kinder-garten

You will need:

Access to outside with some plants (a local park, meadow, woods, your back garden or even a window box!)
Plain paper (scrap, or recycled packing paper or card would be fine)
Pens
Double-sided sticky tape/PVA glue (optional: if you want to keep your leaf art)
IMAGINATION!

How to:

Get outside and explore! Have fun and collect leaves – as many different shapes, sizes and colours as you can find (this was my boys' favourite part and they also picked up some flowers, feathers, sticks and pebbles for good measure).

Once you have gathered enough leaves (or your little legs are worn out), head back home for a drink and a gingerbread man (or is that just us?), then lay out all your leaves and have a good look at them (we laid ours out on a large sheet of white paper so that we could all position the leaves at the same time – like a kind of communal canvas).

Let your imagination loose and see what shapes leap out at you. Some leaves instantly suggested certain creatures to me, but others (like the bunny) were revealed after we played with the leaves in different combinations.

Add a few pen or pencil marks (if needed) to make your

interpretation more obvious.

For us, this was a fast, process art activity and we didn't keep the pictures, but if you think you will want to, press the leaves or iron them first and then use double-sided tape or PVA glue to stick them to the paper. Or you could just take a photo...

Gude - Hodge Podge Craft

(Jude-with-a-G) I'm a theme-park-loving, paper-folding, stationery addicted mum to two small boys. Crafting makes me happy and Hodge Podge Craft is a place to share easy crafting activities and projects for and with the kids, including cross-stitch & origami tutorials and easy gift ideas. http://www.hodgepodgecraft.com/

Clothesline Matching

Fine Motor

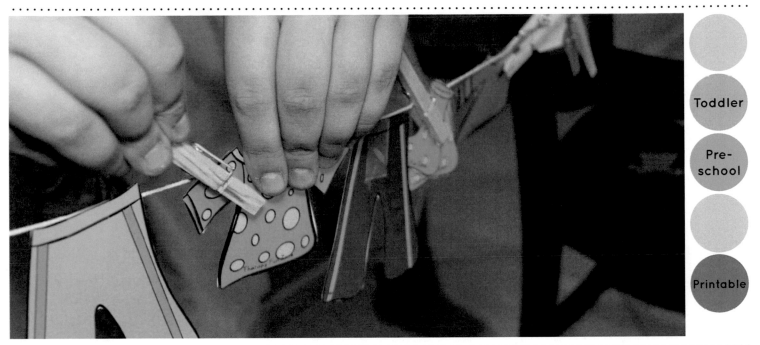

You will need:

Clothesline (string, ribbon, yarn)
Play clothes (printable)
Clothespins
Two chairs to hang the clothesline

How to:

A simple and fun activity for young kids is hanging play clothes on a clothesline. This activity happens to be great for targeting fine motor skills, finger strength and visual perception. It is a lot harder than you think to hold clothes up to the clothesline, get them in the right position while pinching open a clothespin, and lining the clothespin up the right way in order to get it clipped onto the clothes. There are a lot of skills happening at one time.

To play the activity, you need a clothesline (which can be a string, ribbon, twine, or yarn), some play clothes (which can be doll clothes or the clothes printable), and clothespins. I use two chairs to hold my clothesline in place and I tie the string to the backs of the chairs. If you are using real doll clothes, then you can hang some up and have the child match like clothes to like clothes (ie shirts to shirts) or colors to colors. I am using the printable clothes so I printed out two copies of the clothes and attached one to the string with tape so that the child could match the exact same piece of clothes and hang it on top of the matching clothes.

This is a great way to use some large movements while working on visual discrimination and fine motor skills. You could have kids take turns and work together to match the clothes, or you could divide the clothes and have them compete against each other. I will often place the clothes in one area away from the child and they have to go get another piece of clothes to hang up. It is also a great activity to get kids to move into the positions that they need to, such as squatting to pick up clothes, crawling to get some clothes, or using animal walks to go get more clothes.

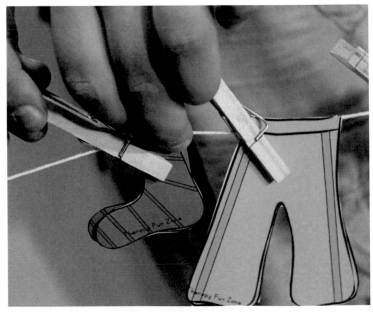

Tonya Cooley - Therapy Fun Zone

Tanya is a Pediatric Occupational Therapist and mother of two. Therapy Fun Zone is about fun and creative activities that help with developing skills. The work involved in development is best when it involves play and fun.
http://therapyfunzone.net/blog/

Sensory Shaving Foam Painting

Fine Motor, Sensory, Color Learning

Toddler

Pre-school

Kinder-garten

You will need:

A container
Shaving foam
A variety of coloured paints
Glitter (optional)
Paper
Straw

How to:

Fill your container with shaving foam. You want a good coverage in the container so aim for around an inch thick or more.

Squirt droplets of paint into the shaving foam; using lots of brightly coloured paint will make this look more effective. You can also add a sprinkle of glitter if you wish.

Take the straw and use it to explore the shaving foam. Pull the straw through the drops of paint and look on as beautiful multicoloured swirls start to appear in the shaving foam.

As well as enjoying this sensory painting activity, you can also go on to capture the beautiful swirls by pushing a sheet of paper down onto the colourful shaving cream. Remove the paper, scrape off the shaving cream and leave it to dry. You will then be left with a beautiful piece of artwork.

Amy Powell - Learning and Exploring Through Play

Learning & Exploring Through Play
Inspiring Ideas for Little Learners

Amy is a stay-at-home mom with a background in education. She is passionate about children learning through their play and that is the driving force behind her blog. Learning and Exploring Through Play is full of inspiring arts, crafts and sensory play ideas for children. http://learningandexploringthroughplay.com/

Muddy Pigs Craft

Sensory, Play Recipes, Imagination Play

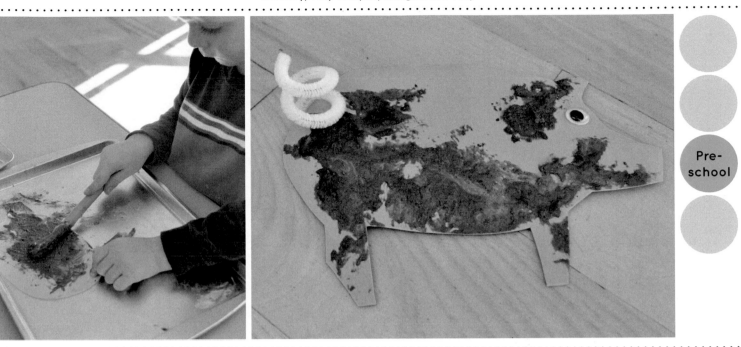

Pre-school

You will need:

Pink foam
Googly eye
White or pink chenille stem
Shaving cream
Brown paint
Small handful of sand
Hot glue and glue gun
Paint palette and brushes
Pen
Scissors
Small bowl for mixing sensory paint

How to:

One thing I can always count on when it comes to teaching preschool is how much my students love anything farm themed. These muddy pigs are no exception.

The pig shape is foam, which will hold the paint recipe better than paper, cardstock or even poster board. Students mix together their own sensory paint recipe to paint their pigs all muddy. The steps are simple, and your preschooler is sure to enjoy this intentionally messy craft.

Step 1 - Begin by cutting out a pig shape from the cardstock. I printed a pig shape off the internet, cut it out, and then traced it onto the foam. At this point, you can either cut the foam yourself, or you can have your preschooler do it.

Step 2 - Invite your preschooler to mix up the sensory paint. Pour a dollop of brown paint into a small bowl with a preschooler sized handful of sand, and then fill the rest of the bowl with shaving cream. Use a spoon or paintbrush to mix well.

My preschoolers loved this step. The sensory paint made of brown paint, sand and shaving cream will create the neatest paint once dried. It will feel sandy to the touch, but will also be slightly fluffy. It will dry to look just like real mud. (And if your shaving cream is completely unscented, it might smell a little like real mud, too!)

Step 3 - Invite your preschooler to use the above mixture to paint mud on the foam pig. Some of my preschoolers painted only the hooves, belly, and snout of the pig, while others painted very, very muddy pigs, covering them in their entirety. Allow to dry.

Step 4 - Once the "mud" is dry, glue on a googly eye.

Step 5 - To make the twirly pig tail, have your preschooler wrap a chenille stem around a pencil to make a spiral. I used a six-inch piece, but it can be longer or shorter. I find that six inches is a good length for preschoolers to properly form their own spiral. Glue to the pig.

Play and Enjoy!

We played with these muddy pigs during our farm theme. The students played with them during block play, making fences and corrals for the pigs. They were used like puppets to retell stories from the books we read. These muddy pigs are a simple craft but one that pairs nicely with other thematic activities.

Sarah Punkoney, MAT - Stay At Home Educator

Sarah is an educator and stay at home mother of four. Stay at Home Educator, focuses on using educational research to create a careful balance of play-based and skills-based learning activities for toddlers and preschoolers. Sarah loves sushi, mountain biking and Krav Maga, hates back massages and hopes to one day climb Machu Picchu.
http://stayathomeeducator.com/

Birthday Cake Play Dough Recipe

Fine Motor, Sensory, Play Recipes

Toddler

Pre-school

Kinder-garten

You will need:

1 ½ cups of sprinkle cake mix, such as Duncan Hines Confetti Cake
1 cup flour
¾ cup water
3 teaspoons cream of tartar
½ cup salt
3 tablespoons coconut (or vegetable) oil

How to:

This recipe is the result of my misunderstanding one of the little girls in my preschool class. She began talking about "Birthday Cake Play Dough" and by the time I realized she was talking about the props she would play with (candles, cupcake tins) and not the type of play dough, this recipe had already been invented in my head.

This play dough is basically made like any other Cream of Tartar/ heated on the stove play dough except for one "trick": despite the fact that I have it listed first on the ingredients list, the cake mix should be added last. Mixing in the cake mix last keeps the sprinkles from mixing into the liquid too much and turning the play dough gray!

Put all ingredients except cake mix into a saucepan and heat, blending well. Add cake mix and stir until thickened. Knead for a few moments until cooled.

A tip for making play dough with very young children:

Because the cream of tartar will be doing its magical work, you can actually heat all ingredients first, and then turn off the stove to let your child "help." He or she will still feel the heat of the stove and be able to mix, without such a high risk of burning him or herself. The play dough should still firm up nicely. And if not, play dough is very forgiving in general – add in a little more flour or reheat!

Birthday cake play dough smells great and weathers the elements pretty well (it can be left out for longer than many play doughs because it stays so soft.) Cutting, kneading and rolling the play dough into snakes or small balls are all great ways to gain hand strength and practice fine motor skills!

Jill Morgenstern - Do Try This at Home

Jill Morgenstern has a Master's Degree in teaching reading and 13 years of teaching experience. She writes about her family and the ridiculous at http://DoTryThisAtHome.net

Rainbow Scented Beans

Fine Motor, Sensory, Play Recipes, Color Learning

Pre-school

You will need:

6 Pounds White Northern beans
Neon liquid food dye
Rubbing alcohol
Essential oils for scents
Plastic zipped bags

How to:

This is a fun way to play with scents and touch at the same time. Kids will love digging through these gorgeous and sweet smelling beans!

To start, separate the beans into gallon size plastic zipped bags using 2 cups of beans in each bag. You can use as many bags as you'd like. Each one represents a different color or scent that you will be making.

Squirt 15 drops of food dye into the bags and pour 1/4 cup of rubbing alcohol on top of the beans and colors. The alcohol enables the dye to spread through to all the beans and allows the vibrant hues to be absorbed by the pale beans. Since it evaporates quickly, your beans will be ready for playtime within a few hours.

Mix the colors together by squishing the bags in your hands. This part of the prep is also fun for closely-monitored children, as they can rub the beans together through the bag and watch the color spread from bean to bean.

When the colors are all mixed together, you can get started on the scents. Add a few drops of your favorite essential oils to the mixes. You can match colors to smells or get creative with your own combinations. We used scents like Lemon, Peppermint and Lavender. The oils are extremely fragrant so you can do a whole bag with minimal drops of the oils.

When the colors and scents are all mixed the way you want them, spread the beans on cookie sheets. They will need to dry in open air for a few hours to allow the color to set. The alcohol must evaporate completely during this time. If this step is skipped the colors may bleed onto your children's hands and clothing.

There are SO many ways that your kids can enjoy these colorful beans. In sensory bins, making mosaics or even through tube play. Regardless of the method, they are sure to have fun learning about colors and smells at the same time.

Holly Homer & Rachel Miller - Kids Activities Blog

Holly Homer & Rachel Miller are on a mission to reveal the kitchen junk drawer as a place of inspiration for kids' art, crafts, games and learning activities. Kids Activities Blog exists because parenting is fun!
http://kidsactivitiesblog.com/

Sticky Shapes Fun

Fine Motor, Gross Motor, DIY Toys, Busy Bags, Imagination Play, Color Learning, Math, Counting, Shapes, Size Sorting

Toddler

Pre-school

Kinder-garten

You will need:

Contact paper or transparent self adhesive roll
Large sheets of foam mats in different colors
Scissors

How to:

The best toys are those that are designed by the kids themselves. And when the game is a perfect quiet time play... it means hours of fun and adventure!

We used just two materials to build a game that children can play in so many ways. It is perfect for all ages, be it toddler or big kid. You can use it as a learning tool too.

Spread a sheet of contact paper with sticky side up on a surface. You can turn the opposite ends inwards for it to stick or you can use tape.

Cut the foam sheets into different shapes. If you have an older child, let them do the cutting. You can make red squares in different sizes, blue triangles in all shapes and sizes, yellow circles, purple rectangles and so on. Pile them up in a tumbler or in a bowl.

Time to play!

Different Ways To Play

Shape sorting:
This is a perfect game to teach your child about shapes. If you have used different colored mats to make the same shape then asking them to sort a single shape can be fun. You can also show them how to combine different shapes to make a bigger shape. For example, four triangles make a square or two triangles make a larger triangle.

Color Sorting:
Let the children sort out the different colors and put them either side by side or in towers.

3D Figures:
The shapes can stand too. Help your child build little cubes and prisms. Ask them what else they can make.

Simple Math Games:
This is a fantastic game to help your child learn some math too. You can teach them to count, learn sequences (one red, two blue, one red, two blue), skip count or even bar graphs!

Scissor Cutting Skills For Older Children:
This is a perfect game to play when you have little toddlers with bigger kids. You can ask the older kid to cut the shapes. This can help them master some cutting skills. Little children love to watch peers and copy. The older child can show them how to build and the younger one can try and copy.

Aysh Siddiqua - Words n Needles

Aysh is a biotechnologist turned stay-at-home mum to three little ones. She is a self-confessed crochet addict, a lace tatter and a craft lover. She writes about her positive parenting hacks, craftsy adventures and crochet projects at Words n Needles.

Glow In The Dark Slime

Gross Motor, Play Recipes

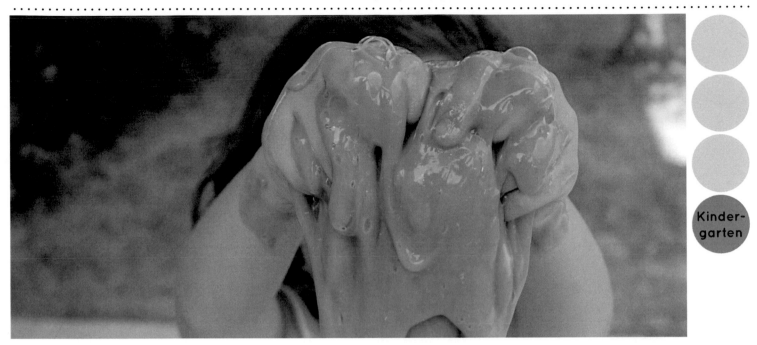

Kinder-
garten

You will need:

1/4 cup of corn syrup
1/4 cup of glow-in-the-dark acrylic paint
1/4 cup of glitter glue (we used purple)
1/4 cup of water
1 teaspoon of Borax

How to:

Slime is something that all kids love. It's the ooie gooie-ness of it that seems like it shouldn't be allowed. The great thing is, the slime is more than okay to play with! Kids will have fun running it through their hands and watching it ooze!

We do measure off our ingredients, but you can adjust them as needed to make yours a slightly different consistency. It is not an exact science.

To start out, mix the glue, paint, water and syrup in a disposable cup. When you are done stirring, it will look like slightly milky water. Your slime will not start to solidify until you add the borax.

Be sure to use careful supervision when you get out the borax. It is not safe if ingested, so be sure you keep all eyes on the kiddos to be sure no one eats the slime or accidentally gets some borax in their mouths during the mixing. Best practice may be to let the kids do the stirring until it comes time to add the borax. At that point mom or dad can take over.

When your mixture looks like watery milk, add the teaspoon of borax. Stir continuously for a few minutes. The glue and borax will combine to make a polymer as you stir. The corn syrup and paint add tension making this slimier than other borax polymer recipes! As all kids know, the slimier - the better!

When the slime is ready, take it outside. It can easily stain carpet or clothing, so this will always be something you want to use outdoors. If you use it at nighttime you can see the slime glow!

When you are done playing store the slime in an airtight jar so you can use it again! Your kids will love playing with this over and over again!

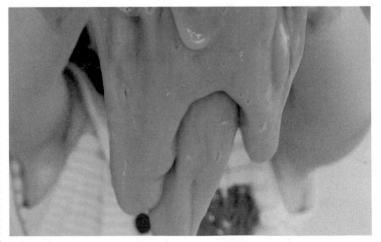

Holly Homer & Rachel Miller - Kids Activities Blog

Holly Homer & Rachel Miller are on a mission to reveal the kitchen junk drawer as a place of inspiration for kids' art, crafts, games and learning activities. Kids Activities Blog exists because parenting is fun.
http://kidsactivitiesblog.com/

DIY Shape and Color Sorting Toy

Fine Motor, DIY Toys, Color Learning, Shapes, Size Sorting

Toddler

Pre-
school

You will need:

Wooden shapes in six different sizes and/or shapes
Acrylic paints in rainbow colors, white and black.
E-6000 glue (to be handled by adults only)
A metal tin, or a shallow cardboard box
Jar caps
Paintbrush

How to:

This DIY sorting game is engaging and educational. It teaches fine motor skills, color, shapes and a little bit of size. Children who know how to paint can assist in the creation, or it can be created by older siblings or caregivers. I used upcycled supplies whenever possible, making this an eco-friendly choice as well.

Paint the inside of your tin black.
It's best to have a few smaller jar lids, like lids from baby food jars, and a larger one like salsa jar lids. Paint the small jar lids in the colors of the rainbow. Paint the large one white.

If you have primary colors of paints, you can mix your own colors. This adds an extra element of learning when making it with children.

Choose a shape and size to match each color (besides the white) and paint a few of them accordingly. For example, small hearts are red, large hearts are purple, small squares yellow, etc. I did nine of the smaller ones, and five of the larger ones to allow for missing pieces.

Glue the jar lids open side up onto the cover of your tin. Make sure to allow enough space around the edge so the lid can close. Allow to dry for 24 hours. Since E-6000 is an industrial strength glue, it should be handled by adults only.

Store the pieces inside the tin and place them into the white lid for play. Children can now sort the shapes according to color, and name the shapes while playing. The white backdrop allows the child to find the right color easily. The black inside of the tin keeps it looking as fresh as possible. It makes a great travel toy as it is self-contained and will provide hours of entertainment.

Menucha - Moms & Crafters

Hi! I'm Menucha, the lone force behind Moms and Crafters. I'm a mom to a mischievous little toddler, freelance graphic designer, jewelry artist, and chocolate lover! I blog full time, and craft in my spare time.
http://momsandcrafters.com/

The Colors of My Feelings

Fine Motor

Toddler

Pre-school

You will need:

Paper
Pens, paint or colored pencils
A list of feelings
Something circular to trace

How to:

Children will love to explore their feelings with The Colors of My Feelings activity. Putting colors to emotions has been going on for centuries. After all, some people believe that the expression "green with envy" goes back to ancient Greece. It makes sense to use colors to help children express their feelings and to understand the feelings of other people.

Here is a list of suggestions for the color of feelings:
Green: good ideas, happy, friendly
Red: bad ideas, angry, unfriendly
Blue: sad, uncomfortable
Yellow: frightened
Black: facts, truth
Orange: questions
Brown: comfortable, cozy
Purple: proud
Color Combinations: confused

It is important to remember that these are suggestions. For colors to have a true personal meaning, each person has to define their own colors. Every time we do this activity the children choose different colors for their feelings.

Target Skills: Fine Motor, Empathy, Drawing Skills

Talk about different feelings. Make a list with the child. Have the child trace and fill colored circles on a piece of paper. You can have the circles already drawn for the child on the paper if needed.

Ask what feeling each color represents to them. Have them draw the expression on the colored circle that matches the feeling that they chose. Use a mirror or have the children observe each other as they model the feeling.

Have the child pay attention to the way the arms and legs are drawn, paying attention to whether the body matches the expression. Ask the child to mimic with their face and body what they drew.

When the drawing is complete, talk about when they felt angry, sad, confused, etc. Problem solve what they could do when they have those feelings.

Talk about when they experienced someone else being angry, confused, proud, happy, etc. Why do they think that the other person felt that way? Keep the picture they made as a reference. Check back with them after a few weeks. Do the colors still match the feelings for them?

Have them use the feelings characters to tell a story. It can be about a pretend situation or you can guide them to tell a story about a real life event.

I always love to see the drawings that the kids create. These colorful feelings people are so lively and expressive.

Shelah - Mosswood Connections

Shelah Moss is an autism consultant, tutor and mother. Her goal in life is to continue to learn and teach while having fun. http://mosswoodconnections.com/

Chamomile Play Dough

Sensory, Play Recipes

Toddler

Pre-school

Kinder-garten

You will need:

2 cups plain flour (we used gluten-free)
4 tablespoons cream of tartar
1 cup salt
2 cups strong chamomile tea
2 tablespoons cooking oil

How to:

Play Dough is a favorite play medium at our place. I love making it and both of my girls love playing with it. I first made this recipe when my eldest was 26 months. She is now four years old and still loves it!

This play dough is really great for when you need your little one to calm down. It can be presented and used in so many different ways, such as with simple play dough toys, cookie cutters, animal figurines...the list goes on!

For this invitation to play, I made up some chamomile play dough and collected a few flowers and overgrown herbs from our garden. My eldest daughter added some glass beads (she was beyond the mouthing stage!) and sticks, her scissors and a rolling pin. She came up with some really gorgeous creations and the more she rolled, crushed and cut the herbs and flowers, the more beautiful it smelled!

To create a batch of this calming, chamomile play dough for your little one just follow these simple directions:

Step 1: Mix all ingredients in a saucepan.

Step 2: Stir over medium heat for 3-5 minutes or until the mixture congeals.
Step 3: Remove from heat and dump on a lightly floured bench and cool slightly.
Step 4: Once cool enough to touch knead until smooth.

Store in an airtight container.

Victoria Milne McInnes - Squiggles and Bubbles

Victoria is a trained early childhood teacher who is lucky enough to be a stay-at-home- and play-Mum to her two beautiful girls, Squiggles (24months) and Bubbles (4years). When her schedule permits, she blogs about the activities she does with her girls in the hopes of inspiring other parents to engage in simple, meaningful play with their children. http://www.squigglesandbubbles.blogspot.com/

Magnetic Fishing Game

Sensory, Gross Motor, DIY Toys

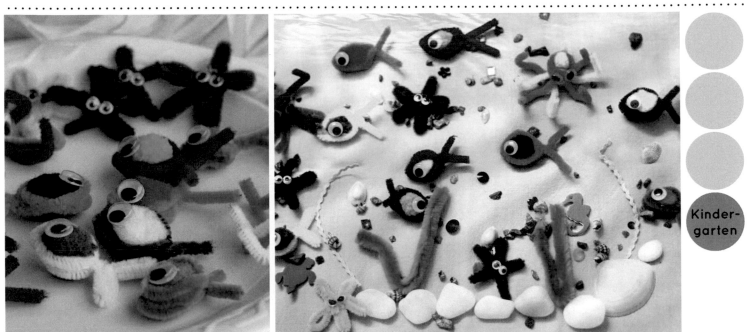

Kinder-garten

You will need:

Pipe cleaners
Assorted pompoms
Craft sticks
Googly eyes
Magnets
Satin ribbon
Sea shells
Assorted sequins
Glue gun
Desert sand (optional)

How to:

Games provide important skills for young children, plus they are fun too. They also help teach children necessary life skills, such as cooperation, critical-thinking and motor control. It's amazing what you can make when you have the right materials. We love making our own toys at home. We have made an ice cream catching game, the snakes and ladders and many more. Not only are DIY games low cost, they give children a sense of achievement. Here is an easy project for you to try at home.

Objective - catch as many fish as you can within a minute. The one who catches the most is the winner.

Encourages:
Movement, precision, gross motor skills, spatial coordination & sporting spirit

The Fish
Take a pipe cleaner in any bright colour, fold it in half, twist at the end to form the tail fin, and then roll the other side around your thumb to form a circular hole. Push a pom pom inside the circle.

To secure the pom pom, you can add additional glue; craft glue or a glue gun works best. Stick a large googly eye to make the fish eye. Make many fishes in different colors.

The Octopus
You'll need 4 pipe cleaners; 2 each of the same colour. Fold the pipe cleaners in half and then twist them all to form a ball like structure with 8 legs. Bend the legs upwards. Stick on two large googly eyes.

The Star Fish
Twist a pipe cleaner in a zig zag – VVVVV with 5 points. Join the ends and press or twist to keep them in place. Stick on two small googly eyes.

Fishing Rod
Make a fishing rod using a satin ribbon that is stuck onto a craft stick at one end and has a small circular magnet at the other end. Make one each for every player.

To Play
Create a fun setup in a blue tub or on a bed spread. Place some sand, some decorative stones, and some sea shells.

We added in some colorful sequins to jazz it up. The magnet will help you 'catch' some pipe cleaner fish. Whoever catches the most fish in a minute wins.

Shruti - Artsy Craftsy Mom

Shruti Bhat wears many hats throughout her day - Mum to lil P, Wife, Friend, A Scrum Master at work, and the chief dreamer at ArtsyCraftsyMom.com where she shares creative Mum-Tested ideas for children and their parents. http://artsycraftsymom.com/

Throwing Paint

Sensory, Gross Motor, Color Learning

Pre-school

Kinder-garten

You will need:

Paint
Yarn
Clothespin
Box of diaper wipes
Cardboard box

How to:

This activity is every child's dream come true. Instead of paint being confined to paper and brushes, they are finally able to let their imaginations soar, along with the paint! They'll be throwing it across the yard with their hands and using a homemade pendulum that we are going to show you how to make from home. Being allowed to fling paint across the yard is definitely one of the most fun activities our kids have ever tried! Instead of being frowned upon, throwing paint is allowed and encouraged with this fun outdoor activity.

To start out, you will need to create your makeshift pendulum. If you aren't quite up to this much DIY you can also just use your hands to throw the paint that you place on the baby wipes. Both methods are super fun and create different effects on your backyard masterpiece.

To make the pendulum, hammer a nail into a beam or tree branch and tie your string of yarn to it. Attach the clothespin to the end of the yarn and you've got your own DIY pendulum! It's perfect for flinging paint across the yard!

Next, set up a large cardboard box across the way from your string. Let it stand up so it's an easy target for the kids to hit with the paint and diaper wipes.

When everything is set up, you can begin squeezing paint onto diaper wipes. Use the pendulum to fling the paint-filled wipes across the yard and onto the cardboard box! If your kids get bored using the string, you can also see who can throw the wipes farthest across the yard or get the most paint globbed onto the box from afar!

At the end of the day, the box should be bright and colorful, and your hands might be as well! We suggest using washable paint for easy clean up at the water hose when you are done painting. If you allow the cardboard box to dry in the sun, you could even cut it into pieces to hang on the walls of your home. Abstract art at its finest!

Holly Homer & Rachel Miller - Kids Activities Blog

Holly Homer & Rachel Miller are on a mission to reveal the kitchen junk drawer as a place of inspiration for kids' art, crafts, games and learning activities. Kids Activities Blog exists because parenting is fun.
http://kidsactivitiesblog.com/

Heart Mug

Fine Motor

Toddler

Pre-school

Kinder-garten

You will need:

Plain white mug
Sticky back plastic (contact paper)
Porcelain pen

How to:

These heart mugs make great gifts and are easy enough for toddlers or preschool children to make although I'm sure older kids would love them too.

Small children will love the novelty of mark making on a mug using a grown-up pen.

Step 1. Draw a heart shape onto some sticky back plastic. Cut out the middle of the shape.
TIP: Draw around a heart shaped biscuit cutter.

Step 2. Stick the sticky back plastic onto your mug. Make sure the cut out heart is where you would like your heart design to be on your mug. Smooth around the edge of the heart shape to make sure it is flat against the mug. Then get colouring!

Step 3. Scribble using your porcelain pen, making sure you fill in most of the heart shape. (This is the bit small children will love)

Step 4. When you have finished your design, leave it to dry for a minute or two and peel off the sticky back plastic.

Step 5. To make your design permanent and washable follow the oven-firing instructions on the back of the porcelain pen.

These mugs would make great gifts for Valentines day, Mother's Day or a special someone's birthday. They look gorgeous hanging up in the kitchen too.

Louise McMullen - Messy Little Monster

Louise is mum to two gorgeous children, a teacher and writer of 'Messy Little Monster." She loves anything arty and has a fun, creative approach to playing and learning. Messy Little Monster is a kid's activity blog full of art, craft and activity ideas to inspire you. http://www.messylittlemonster.com/

Sparkle Stone Party Place Names

Fine Motor, Literacy, Writing, Learning To Write My Name, ABC

Pre-school

Kinder-garten

You will need:

A large, smooth stone for each party guest
Acrylic paint in bright and light (we used fluorescent!) colours
Newspaper or a plastic/oilcloth sheet
Old clothes or a painting smock (acrylic paint stains)
A paintbrush
Permanent markers in darker and bolder colours
Small self-adhesive crystals - one small sheet for each guest
(you can order these online or look in craft or beauty shops - the ones we used were for sticking onto your nails)

How to:

This is a fun activity for preschoolers to make for a party. If you pre-paint the stones, each party guest can write and decorate his or her name during the party. They look pretty, are a fun way to practise name writing, serve as place names on the table and double-up as party favours!

How to make sparkle stone party place names:
Step 1. Wash your stones and allow them to dry completely.

Step 2. Paint them at least a day ahead of your party, with at least 2 coats of acrylic paint, allowing each coat a couple of hours to dry and the final coat to dry overnight. We painted ours different colours, but you could do them all the same (or one colour for girls and another for boys), whatever you choose. My only advice is to choose brighter and lighter colours, as we found the darker colours (like purple), did not give enough contrast to the letters later on and were harder to read.

Step 3. On the day of your party, give each guest a painted stone and let them write their own name on it with a Sharpie. If they are not able to write their whole name yet, they could just write the initial letter, or of course you could write it for them*.

Step 4. Give each guest a small sheet of self-adhesive crystals to decorate their name or initial. They may want to make the whole name sparkle, or just the first letter. They may want to use the crystals to add extra designs (flowers, butterflies, polka dots, arrows). This part is great for developing fine motor skills.

Step 5. Encourage them to use their imagination (there is no right or wrong here) and to make each stone completely personal to them.

Once everyone is finished, enjoy the rest of the party and remind your guests to take their special sparkle stone home with them as a favour at the end.

*You might want to provide an example stone with your name on it (sticking crystals is quite a calming activity and great to counteract the stress of organising a party for pre-schoolers)!

Gude - Hodge Podge Craft

Hello! I'm Gude (Jude-with-a-G) I'm a theme-park-loving, paper-folding, stationery addicted mum to two small boys. Crafting makes me happy and Hodge Podge Craft is a place to share easy crafting activities and projects for and with the kids, including cross-stitch & origami tutorials and easy gift ideas. http://www.hodgepodgecraft.com/

Sidewalk Chalk Paint

Play Recipes, DIY Toys, Imagination Play, Color Learning

Toddler

Pre-school

Kinder-garten

You will need:

Old chalk
Plastic sandwich bags
Disposable bowls
Hammer
Water
Brushes

How to:

Everyone loves sidewalk chalk! Kids can spend hours outside covering a concrete patio, driveway or yes, even the sidewalk in colorful chalk drawings. The only problem with sidewalk chalk are the stubby bits of chalk left over when the sticks are worn down...or thrown back into the bucket with a little too much force.
So what do you do with all the leftover bits and too short pieces? Recycle it into paint, of course!

Obviously I didn't invent sidewalk chalk paint–there's a bunch of recipes out there you could use. But here's how it worked for us. Separate your chalk stubs into colors, then fill a sandwich bag with one color of chalk scraps. Seal the bag then gently smash with a hammer. You want to crush the chalk but not tear holes in the bag. You'll get the best results if you can turn the chalk into fine powder, but don't drive yourself crazy. Some lumps won't matter for an art medium that's only going to get washed away with a garden hose later.

Next, dump the chalk powder into a disposable bowl. Add a tablespoon of water at a time and stir–you can use a brush to stir the mixture. The amount of water you need will depend on the amount of chalk you have. It won't be like real paint–you're shooting for something like melted ice cream. Thinner "paint" will still work, but it may not show very dark until it dries.

Repeat these steps for each color of chalk.

After you're done painting you can save the leftover chalk paint, especially if you mixed it in a disposable bowl you don't need again. Just let the paint dry in the sun for a few hours and it will turn into a chalky patty. Next time you want to paint you just need to add water and stir.

Denise Bertacchi - stlMotherhood

Denise is a Midwestern mom of two boys who loves writing, crafting and playing video games. She's been a freelance newspaper reporter, a online columnist and a blogger. http://stlMotherhood.com/

Ice Painting

Sensory, Play Recipes, Color Learning, Science

Baby

Toddler

Pre-school

Kinder-garten

You will need:

Poster paints
Small pots
Lollipop sticks
Thick paper or card

How to:

Ice painting is so much fun! You get all the freedom and mess of painting but you get to experiment with freezing paint and watch it melt too. I love the bright colours that these ice paints create and the way the ice glides across the paper as it starts to melt.

Making these brightly coloured ice paints is really easy. All you need to do is squeeze some poster paint into some small pots (small yoghurt pots are perfect), put in a lollipop stick and pop them in the freezer.

If you want the colours to be nice and bright like the paints in the picture above don't add any water to the poster paint, just squeeze it into the pots straight from the paint bottles.

Once the paints have frozen, you're ready to get painting!

I would recommend painting on thick paper or card as the paper can get quite soggy!

As the ice starts to melt a little, the paint slides across the paper easily and you end up with really bright bold colours. By painting the colours on top of each other, you can even have a

go at a bit of colour mixing if you make your paints up using the primary colours.

It's great fun breaking the ice as it starts to really melt too. If you add the melted pieces of ice paint to the paper you can create some amazing effects.

Ice painting is a great activity to do collaboratively or on a large scale. You get nice and messy and it's LOTS of fun!

TIP: If babies or young children (that put everything in their mouths) want to get involved, make the ice paints taste safe by freezing water colored with food colouring instead of using poster paint. (See image below)

messylittlemonster

Louise McMullen - Messy Little Monster

Louise is mum to two gorgeous children, a teacher and writer of 'Messy Little Monster." She loves anything arty and has a fun, creative approach to playing and learning. Messy Little Monster is a kid's activity blog full of art, craft and activity ideas to inspire you. http://www.messylittlemonster.com/

Shake It Art

Sensory, Gross Motor, DIY Toys, Color Learning

Toddler

Pre-school

Kinder-garten

You will need:

Ice cube tray
Food colors
Water
Sheet of white or colored paper
A lock it box

How to:

Want your children to play with ice but don't want any mess? We have a fantastic game that is both fun and mess free. Colored ice can be a fun painting tool. Kids love to watch as the colors spread on to the sheet. Sometimes with little toddlers, this can be very messy and it requires a lot of supervision. We came up with a game that can make some really amazing artwork! Put on some music or sing a rhyme together for added fun.

Half-fill the ice cube tray with colored water and freeze them in advance.

Cut scrolls of paper to fit the lock it box. The paper should cover at least two sides of the box from inside. Make sure you are using a box that closes tightly and does not leak. It is possible that the paint will splatter or drip if the box isn't closed well.

Take the frozen cubes out of the tray and keep them ready in a bowl.

Ask your child to put his choice of 2-3 colored ice cubes into the paper lined box. Fit the lid in tightly. Shake the box a few times.

You can say 'Shake shake shake' or like my seven-year-old sings to his sister: 'You shake it, you move it and then tumble it out.'

Open the box and remove the paper gently. Let them admire their artwork before you hang up to air dry. You can display it as it is or let the child get more creative with their art the next day by making a collage on it.

Older kids:
The splatter of paint on the paper can also be used to teach them about color mixing. See what happens when you mix more than three colors together. You can teach them to use the color wheel to identify or guess what colors they will get next.

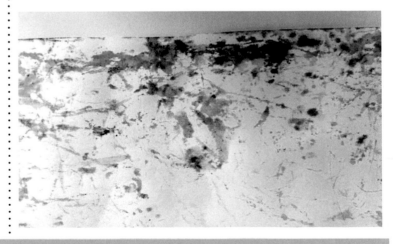

Words n Needles

Aysh Siddiqua - Words n Needles

Aysh is a biotechnologist turned stay-at-home-mum to three little ones. . She is a self-confessed crochet addict, a lace tatter and a craft lover. She writes about her positive parenting hacks, craftsy adventures and crochet projects at Words n Needles. http://wordsnneedles.com/

Fun with a Musical Sensory Bin

Sensory

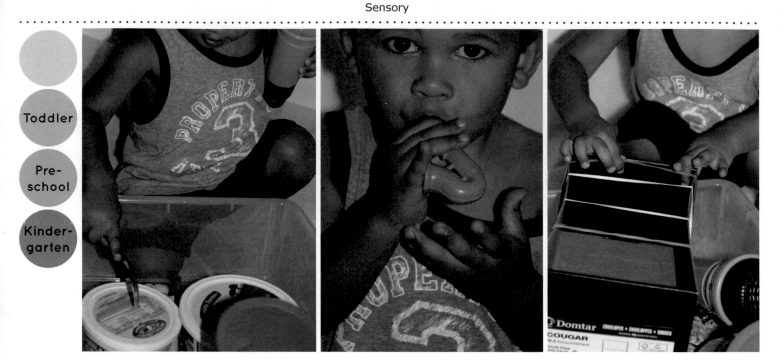

Toddler

Pre-school

Kinder-garten

You will need:

Beans
Rice
Hand drums
Plastic musical crackers
Kazoos
Slide Whistles
Recorder
Microphone
Empty Plastic Containers (of all sizes)

Empty Oatmeal Box
Metal Spoons
Empty Shoe Box
Rubber Bands
Plastic Easter Eggs
Tablecloth

How to:

Children love music. They like to sway and dance to it. They love playing with instruments. They love to sing and love to hear others sing to them. Music and songs can make learning fun and easy for children.

Shannon Wijnker, a music teacher and mother of four, once shared with me, "Children learn best by constructing their own concepts and ideas, and by trial and error. They will learn how to create a variety of sounds. Some of which they will like and some they will decide they don't. Your concept of what is acceptable sound may vary from theirs. But be patient and let them explore. Remember that it's not just about making a beautiful sound, but playing and exploring the concept of sound."

In the spirit of exploration, I created a musical sensory box. I found several items in the party favor section and some in the toy section of my local Dollar Tree store. I picked up a recorder and a toy microphone from the $1 bins at Target.

I placed all the items into a plastic tub and sat the tub on a tablecloth on the floor. I used a tub with sides low enough that my great-nephew could sit in the floor or kneel next to it to play. Jeremiah first experimented by putting beans and rice into different containers. We talked about the different sounds they made. There were different types of whistles and kazoos to play with. We stretched rubber bands around a box and listened to the different sounds they made when we plucked them. He really enjoyed the microphone.

In case you didn't realize it, your voice is an instrument you take with you wherever you go. Jeremiah used the spoons to drum on the different containers. Sometimes he drummed on the tops and sometimes on the bottoms.

Jeremiah was almost 2 years old when I created this Musical Sensory Box. He really enjoyed it and has played with it on more than one occasion. I'm sure he will play with it many more times.

The one thing that I noticed is that some of the whistles didn't work very well. I will probably replace and add some better quality instruments, as I get the money. This was a good place to start and as his interests grow and change we can add to or switch out instruments.

Mama Carmody - Love to Laugh and Learn

I was a stay-at-home mom for 13 years. All I ever wanted to be was a mother and a teacher and I have been blessed and honored to do both. Making learning fun has always been one of my main goals; whether working with my own children or with others'. Having always enjoyed writing, being able to blog about fun educational things to do with children is very rewarding. http://lovetolaughandlearn.com/

Rock Play

Sensory, Imagination Play

Pre-school

Kinder-garten

You will need:

Rocks
Containers
Coasters

How to:

I love providing my children with open-ended opportunities to play, allowing them to create their own learning through play and to express themselves freely. It's amazing how often I will set out a few simple materials and the girls will play with them in ways I had never even imagined.

This little invitation to play grew and expanded over a period of five weeks. It was so successful at home that I even took it into the classroom, where my two- and three- year olds enjoyed it just as much.

Over the five weeks this activity was left out at my house, and the two weeks it was in the classroom the rocks were sorted, shaken in containers, used as play food, used as animals and cars and simply explored. The bamboo coasters became plates, cake stands, cookies, musical instruments, car garages, and again simply explored. In the classroom the children were engaged with the set up all day every day. There was not a moment where at least one child could be seen to be unengaged with the activity and it was similar at home too.

Sometimes it's the simplest activities that are best.

To create this invitation to play I simply placed the rocks in a natural basket, added some bamboo coasters, which just so happen to be my two-year-old's favourite 'toy' at the moment and a lovely wooden container. I left them set up on a low-lying table and stood back and allowed the girls to explore them in their own way.

After a few fights over the container, I added in a tray (packaging from some Christmas decorations). It's interesting because I had to do the same in the classroom-although with more children I added a couple of trays and bowls. That was all that was required on my part-the children did the rest!

Victoria Milne McInnes - Squiggles and Bubbles

Victoria is a trained early childhood teacher who is lucky enough to be a stay-at-home- and play- Mum to her two beautiful girls, Squiggles (24 months) and Bubbles (4years). When her schedule permits she blogs about the activities she does with her girls in the hopes of inspiring other parents to engage in simple, meaningful play with their children. http://squigglesandbubbles.blogspot.com.au/

Pom Pom Ice Cream Shoppe Play

Fine Motor, Sensory, Imagination Play, Color Learning, Math, Counting

Toddler

Pre-school

Kinder-garten

Printable

You will need:

At least 30 large pom poms of various colours (2" ones are the best and look most like scoops of ice cream!) OR a variety of colours of tissue paper crumpled into balls
Small red pom poms for cherries
Paper treat containers or plastic sundae dishes
Plastic ice-cream cones or water-cooler paper cone cups
A large plastic scoop and/or an ice cream scoop
Plastic spoons or ice-cream treat sticks
Coloured rice or confetti for "sprinkles"
A small container or shaker to hold the "sprinkles"
White shredded paper for whipped cream
Ice Cream Shoppe Printable Menu

How to:

Who doesn't love ice cream? And why should it only be seen as a summertime treat?
This anytime-of-the-year sweet sensory bin allows kids to explore different textures (pompoms and rice) while also practising scooping, pouring, and dumping fine-motor skills. It encourages imaginative play and, along with the Ice Cream Shoppe Menu printable, can be used to introduce money concepts, practice counting to 5 and colour matching.

One of the first things to decide is if you want this to be more of a sensory activity or a pretend play activity.

Putting all of the materials into one large tub encourages more open-ended play and exploration. If the materials are presented more like an ice cream sundae making station, with different ingredients in different containers, it encourages a pretend play focus.

Onetime (my preschool-aged son) enjoyed both these set-ups, but REALLY liked "playing Ice Cream Store!" The first thing he went for in the bin was the rice sprinkles shaker! So much fun to shake and pour into treat containers!

Onetime also had a lot of fun scooping and transferring the "ice cream" from cone to treat container and back to the main ice-cream bin. While we were playing, we chatted a lot about different flavours of ice cream and Onetime decided to make a special sundae for Daddy and me. He made sure there were lots of sprinkles for Dad, whipped cream for me, and even a cherry on top!

After lots of time just playing, I brought out the Ice Cream Shoppe Menu. I showed it to my son and talked with him about what a menu is, and what the numbers and dollar signs mean.

Then I asked him if he could match the colours of ice cream on the menu with our pompom ice creams. He enjoyed this and we had fun labelling the different coloured pompoms with fun flavour names like, "Green Chocolate!" and "Fuzzy Blueberry!"

Once all the colours were matched, we looked again at the money amounts and practised our counting. Onetime also felt the need to add sprinkles and a cherry on that last 5-scooper! After an hour's worth of play, we had many different sundae creations for various family members. What a fun and educational morning!

Sue Lively - One Time Through

Sue is a behaviour therapist, turned elementary school teacher, turned stay-at-home mom. On One Time Through, she shares her adventures of creating, observing, and celebrating life and parenthood with her favourite little guy, her preschool-aged son "Onetime!" http://onetimethrough.com/

I-Spy Counting Bottles

Sensory, DIY Toys, Counting

Baby

Toddler

Pre-school

Kinder-garten

You will need:

Clear bottles
A filler of some sort (I used maize rice. But again, whatever you want to use. I just found a plain color does the counting objects justice)
Small objects to place in the bottles.
Number stickers (I used foam numbers)

How to:

Counting skills can be acquired through play, and they usually are. These easy make-it-yourself counting I-spy bottles are great for counting, and they can be a frugal teaching tool too!

Now, involve the kids in the next steps: adding the small objects, using a tweezer, and the filler, using a funnel and spoon/scoop. Although involving the kids with filling the bottles will make the process take twice as long, it is a great fine motor skills and hand -eye coordination activity.

You could glue the lids onto the bottles to keep the kids from throwing everything out, but I did not do this because my sensory seeking daughter (4.5 years) wanted to explore more. So we did the following: we threw one bottle at a time out into the sensory bin, and let her explore for a while. Then we packed it away again, and threw out another bottle.

With my son (2 years), I kept the filler in the bottles for exploring the safe way, since the small objects could be hazardous. Both of them enjoyed playing and learning with these bottles.

A few ideas on how to play:
"Spying" the objects you can see
Playing with a friend the I-spy game using the bottle (I spy an object that is red and starts with a "b" etc.)
Counting the objects in each bottle
Finding the same type of object in a bottle, or use two bottles with the same objects and add them together (older children might like to do a sum on paper)
Exploring the object names: find two objects that sounds the same(start with the same letter or rhymes)
Make a graph on paper about the objects you can see

Using concrete objects make mathematical concepts "come to life", so to speak. Use the I-spy counting bottles and make learning fun for your kids! AND did I mention what a great traveling toy this can be? When the lids are secured, it is a no mess toy, that can be played over and over with in the car. Remember it for your next trip!

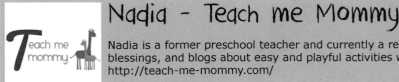

Nadia - Teach me Mommy

Nadia is a former preschool teacher and currently a remedial therapist for elementary students. She is a mommy to 2 blessings, and blogs about easy and playful activities with the aim to teach as well as DIY projects for mommy. http://teach-me-mommy.com/

Easy Egg Carton Snake Craft

DIY Toys, Imagination Play

Toddler

Pre-school

Kinder-garten

You will need:

Egg carton
Paint
Paintbrush
Glue
Googly eyes
Pipe cleaner
Sponge (optional)
Red paper, craft foam, or felt

How to:

Doing recycled crafts with kids is a great way to teach them the importance of reusing what we have and taking care of our Earth. It's also a fun way to get them to think creatively and 'outside-the-box' by turning something like an empty egg carton, cardboard tube, empty food container, and so on into a car, ladybug, or wherever their imagination takes them. Here is a fun way to turn an empty egg carton into a snake that kids can have fun playing with when finished.

Cut a cardboard egg carton in half. Paint one of the halves (or both if you'd like) with a color of choice. We painted ours orange. Let dry. Add a second coat of paint.

Sponge paint the egg carton with 1-2 different colors. We used yellow and red. The easiest way to do this is to put a small amount of paint on a small plate. Lightly dip the sponge into the paint and then dab off the excess right there on the plate. Dab the sponge all over the snake. Repeat with a second color. Let dry.

Cut the egg carton into separate sections. Use a hole punch or an item with a sharp point (adults) to make 2 holes on each egg carton - opposite ends.

String a pipe cleaner through each of the holes. Fold the pipe cleaner ends. Glue on googly eyes and a red tongue made from construction paper, craft foam, or felt.

Now the kids will have a homemade snake toy that can be twisted into different directions! For fun, ask them to make an 'S' shape with it.

Variations: decorate the snake with sequins, buttons, markers, glitter glue, or anything else you can think of.

More egg carton craft ideas: ladybugs, turtles, mini baskets, flowers, and a tray for sorting colors.

Amanda Vasquez - Artsy Momma

Amanda is an 'artsy momma' to 2 kids who love making crafts just as much as she does. Follow their creative journey over on the blog titled Artsy Momma {artsymomma.com}. Besides crafts, they share fun food ideas, hands-on learning activities, mommy DIY, + lots more! If you love handprint art, head over to their Fun Handprint Art blog where you will find hundreds of their projects all made with little hands and feet. http://artsymomma.com/

DIY Small Car Track Busy Bag

Fine Motor, Gross Motor, DIY Toys, Busy Bags, Imagination Play

Toddler

Pre-school

Kinder-garten

You will need:

Wooden domino set – we used Banana's in Pyjamas Wooden Dominoes
Black paint
Wood glue (optional)
Correction tape
A small car

How to:

Does your child get restless whilst waiting for appointments with the doctor? My son has outgrown the toys in our GP's waiting room so I needed something small and portable to keep him amused.

My son loves driving cars around a track but I have been unable to find a car track small enough to fit into my handbag for trips out. Pushing a car along a carpet in a waiting room isn't as much fun as having your own car track. I therefore decided to create one myself. A wooden domino box is the perfect size to fit into a handbag. Fortunately the dominoes I found were curved rather than the standard oblong-shape so when placed together it was easy to create realistic play tracks.

To make the domino pieces resemble a road I mixed wood glue and black paint together and painted the reverse side of each domino piece. I ensured that each edge of the dominoes was covered evenly. Some pieces required a second coat of paint. The wood glue helps the paint to adhere to the wood.

Once the pieces had dried overnight I made white road markings

on each individual domino by using a Tipp-Ex Pocket Mouse.

I also painted the wooden domino box with the same paint and glue mixture so that the track could be stored in it. Once the paint had dried I decorated the wooden box with my son's name and added additional road markings to each side. The domino car track pieces and a small car can be stored in the wooden box to take out with us.

As our domino pieces are not straight the possibilities to create different shaped roads are numerous. A circular race track was perfect for our small racing car and is already proving popular with my son. As the paint may chip off with extended use I will probably add a coat of varnish to prevent this.

Emma Edwards - Adventures of Adam

Adventures Of Adam

During a difficult pregnancy suffering from Hyperemesis Gravidarum (HG) Emma vowed to make every day an adventure once she had recovered. Adventures of Adam is the outcome of completing a 100 day play challenge with her toddler as part of that promise. Emma has a section dedicated to HG friendly play activities so that Mums can still be part of their children's play whilst they are ill. http://adventuresofadam.co.uk/

Hen Farm Junk Play

Fine Motor, Imagination Play

You will need:

Cardboard paper roll insert (use 1 for each hen)
Scraps of colored cardboard paper
Googly eyes or markers
Glue (or glue gun)
Any type of small basket
Artificial grass (or shredded paper)
Egg carton
Plastic easter egg, or egg capsules from Kinder Surprise chocolate

How to:

This simple pretend play game is very easy, and fast to prepare from items found around the home or in a recycle bin.

To make a hen from a cardboard paper roll, cut 3 small triangles for wings and tail from cardboard paper, use any color you have on hand. To create a hen's beak, cut one tiny square from orange paper, and fold it in half. Use any paper based glue or the glue gun to glue all pieces onto the paper roll. To complete your hen, glue a pair of googly eyes or draw eyes by hand above the beak. If you would like to make more than one hen, just repeat all the steps and prepare additional paper rolls in advance. We made it very simple and it took longer for glue gun to heat up than to prepare everything needed to make these hens!

Place the small basket on the table and fill it with grass. This will be the hen's nest. Set the nest, plastic eggs and egg carton on the table and let kids pretend they are running a hen farm.

Plastic egg capsules are just the right size to slide through the paper roll hen and pretend hens are laying eggs. Once the basket (hen's nest) is full with eggs, little farmers can collect eggs and place them in an egg carton for sale!

Placing eggs inside the hen and then transferring to the egg carton is a great way for tiny toddlers to practice fine motor skills.

Tip: You can be very flexible with this game and use what ever you have at home for the nest. Even things like large plastic lids and pieces of torn paper can be used to make a pretend hen's nest.

Mihaela Vrban - Best Toys 4 Toddlers

Mihaela is full time working mother of 2 little girls who keep her busy and creative! She is also a part-time blogger who writes mostly about ways to keep little toddlers and preschoolers busy playing and learning. We believe in our tag line: Playing is serious business! http://www.besttoys4toddlers.com/

Making an Easy Balance Beam

Gross Motor

Toddler

Pre-school

Kinder-garten

You will need:

2x4 boards
String and/or
Painter's tape (or Washi tape)

How to:

Balancing is a very useful skill that is best mastered at a very young age so as to carry you on through the years and into old age. It's not something we like to think about, but it is very important.

Children love to balance along the edge of the curbs, or along the walls when out walking. Children will approach balancing in many different ways. Some will be quite nervous about it and go very slow. Others will be more daring and move with more speed and grace. Some children are more afraid of falling than others. I think it might be easier for younger siblings as they see their older brothers or sisters performing tasks that they think they should be able to do, whereas the eldest child hasn't had someone so close to imitate.

Making a balance beam at home is very easy, doesn't have to cost anything, and will help children with their motor skills at the same time as they are just having plain, old-fashioned fun!

You can make your balance beam as simple or as challenging as you, your children, and your budget is comfortable with.

If you're indoors and looking to make something quick, simply unravel some string and place it along the floor, using a little masking tape to hold the ends in place.
If you have a little more time, you can use painter's tape or Washi tape and make a line or zig-zag on your floor.

Outdoors, children can use the cracks in the sidewalks or curbsides (being careful not to do this without adult supervision). We've made a simple balance beam out of fencing planks that we no longer needed.

The children simply placed them on the ground and walked from one end to the other. If you have a few more, you can raise the "beams" up a little for more of a challenge. These will also make great "roads" later for playing with cars!
If you want something more permanent, you can use tree stumps and logs well-affixed to each other to make a higher beam, and the curve of the logs will add a fun dimension to play.

Whichever type of balance beam you choose to make, be sure to have some fun with your children, too! They'll love to see your skills and joy of spending time with them.

Crystal McClean - Castle View Academy

Crystal is an ex-pat home educating Mama who is passionate about her children, learning, crafting and frugality.
http://www.castleviewacademy.com/

41

Make A Bubblewrap Jellyfish Picture

Fine Motor, Sensory

Toddler

Pre-school

Kinder-garten

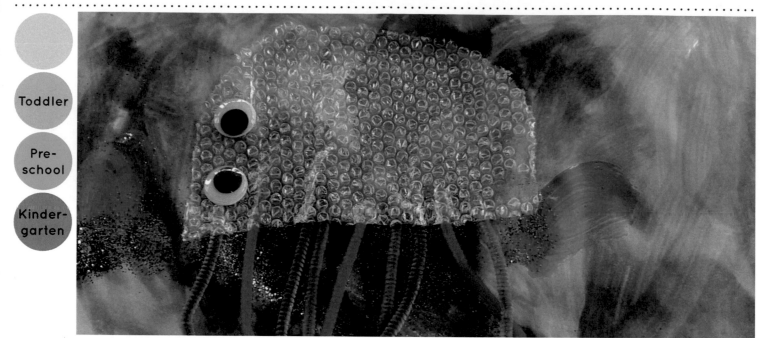

You will need:

Sheet of bubblewrap
White paper
Green and blue paint
Pipe cleaners
Googly eyes
Glitter
Glue
Sticky tape

How to:

I like to encourage my children to get involved in choosing the arts and crafts activities we do all together at home. So when my preschooler asked if we could make some jellyfish pictures, we all sat down along side our "Making Box," (which is full of everyday recyclable items along with the more traditional craft supplies), to chat about how best we could make our pictures. It's great to see them putting their own stamp on to our projects and they often come up with better ideas than I ever could have for some of our projects.

We had a big sheet of bubblewrap in our "Making Box" and we thought this would be ideal to use for the jellyfishes' translucent body. My pre-schooler then suggested pipe cleaners (in different colours) for the wiggly tentacles and of course we had to use our favourite craft material, googly eyes, to finish the pictures off nicely.

We started the activity by diluting blue paint with a dash of water and giving it a good mix. I gave each of my children a paintbrush and a sheet of white paper. They brushed this watery paint all over the whole sheet to create the sea. They then used green paint to add seaweed to the picture. The boys took great care with their painting, but my toddler did get a little distracted and didn't cover her paper. She is only 2, so it was a great effort for her age and concentration levels.

Whilst the paint dried we set to work on the jellyfish. I cut out 3 semi-circle shapes for the bodies from the sheet of bubblewrap and gave one to each of my children. Bubblewrap is quite hard to cut, so this job wouldn't have been suitable for my children aged 2, 4 and 6. The kids then added googly eyes and I helped them to tape on pipe cleaner pieces for the tentacles.

Once the paint was dry, I then got each of my children to spread glue over the bottom of the picture and they sprinkled glitter over this to create the sandy sea bed. Now I don't tend to get glitter out too often, as it can result in trouble when it's mixed with a toddler. It was worth it in this instance, as it really helped to finish off the picture, and my daughter didn't cause too much mayhem with it this time.

Nicola Simpson - Crafty Kids at Home

Nicola is a children's arts and crafts writer and mummy to two sons and one daughter aged 2-7. She grew up in the UK, but now lives by the sea in Ireland. Her kids adore making things and getting messy and she loves to come up with new ideas for them all to do together at home. http://www.craftykidsathome.com/

Hand And Finger Strengthening

Milestone Encouragement, Fine Motor, Life Skills

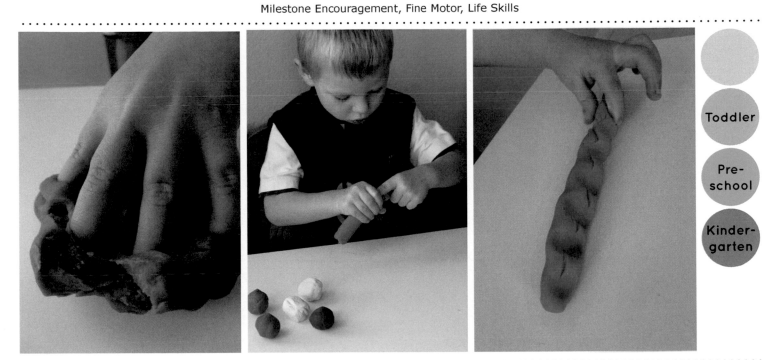

Toddler

Pre-school

Kinder-garten

You will need:

Play dough
Small objects like a Lego, marble, pen cap, etc.

How to:

As children grow, their hands and fingers have to do all sorts of complicated and challenging tasks from buttoning their shirts to writing their names. Many everyday skills in life require fine motor abilities. Usually children develop stronger hands and fingers and fine tune their small motor skills naturally through normal play.

Occasionally, a child struggles with underdeveloped muscles or poor body awareness and coordination. An easy way to strengthen hand control is through manipulating play dough. Here are four specific exercises, though the possibilities are endless.

Have the child roll the play dough into a cylinder and place it in their palm. With the opposite hand, insert a single finger into the play dough. Encourage them to keep their finger straight as they work the individual finger against the resistance of the play dough. Repeat with all five fingers and then switch hands.

Completely surround a small object with play dough. Using their hands in conjunction, have the child find and "free" the object from the play dough.

Roll the play dough into a large ball and place it on the table.

Have the child place the tips of all five fingers in the dough and slowly spread them wide in order to increase gross opposition skills. Then have the child go in the opposing direction, pulling the flattened dough into the center, creating a cone shape.

Make a long "rope" with the play dough. Instruct the child to pinch all along the rope, squeezing the index finger and thumb together till they nearly touch. This develops a stronger pincer grasp.

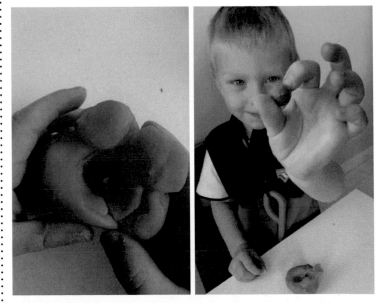

Julie Nixon - My Mundane and Miraculous Life

Julie is a frazzled mom of two tornadoes, one with special sensory needs. As a dorky second-generation homeschooler, she writes about learning and play, natural living and matters of the heart. She serves an astounding God that radically saved her. http://www.mymundaneandmiraculouslife.com/

DIY Window Gel Clings

Sensory, Play Recipes, Imagination Play, Science

You will need:

Four cups of boiling water
Six packets of unflavored gelatin (about 43 grams)
Food coloring
Glitter, Googly Eyes, and/or Beads, if desired. (Please note: These may be a choking hazard for very small children.)
Toothpicks
One large baking sheet with a rim
Cookie cutters
Spatula

How to:

Make window gel clings using just three edible ingredients. This is a safe and fun creative activity for kids of all ages. You can customize the colors and shapes for whatever holiday or season you want.

Add gelatin all at once to the hot water. Use a whisk to stir to make sure it all dissolves. Spoon out any bubbles. Pour the mixture into the baking sheet. You want it to be about a quarter of an inch thick (½ – ¾ cm). It doesn't have to be exact, but make sure it is level.

Once the gelatin mixture has cooled a bit (10-15 minutes), have fun dropping food coloring into the gel and swirling it around with a toothpick. For an extra flare, sprinkle glitter over the top or add a few beads or googly eyes. You probably only have about 30 minutes before the gelatin starts to harden, so don't dawdle!

When you are done decorating, let the gelatin harden for at least a couple of hours. Leaving it out uncovered overnight yields the best results. Once it has set, use cookie cutters to cut out shapes or cut out your own shapes using a butter knife.

Use a spatula to carefully lift the gel shapes out of the pan. Don't worry if they tear because you can simply mold them back together. Stick them onto the windows and enjoy!

Because the gelatin is so viscous, you can decorate each corner differently and the colors/glitter won't run into each other. Be sure to help your child observe how the window gels thin out and evaporate over time. They start out squishy and thick, but within a week or so they will have lost enough water that only dry, paper-thin shapes remain stuck to the window.

Note: You probably won't be able to take these jellies off the window and put them back on more than a few times before they tear beyond repair. They are more delicate than the window gels available at the store.

Crystal Chatterton - The Science Kiddo

Crystal is a homeschooling mom of two blondies. After giving up an academic career in chemistry to stay home with her kids, she launched The Science Kiddo to focus on doing science experiments with her children. She blogs about science activities for kids, early childhood science education, homeschool, and urban living.
http://www.sciencekiddo.com/

Soda Bottle Rainbow

Fine Motor, Color Learning

Toddler

Pre-
school

Kinder-
garten

You will need:

Tissue paper (red, orange, yellow, green, blue, purple)
Empty plastic 2 litre bottle (each 2 litre bottle makes two rain-bows)
Paper plate
Cotton balls
Clear tape
Paint brush
White glue

How to:

We turned an old 2 liter soda bottle into a beautiful rainbow that seems to glow when held in the light. I love using things around the house to make art; it saves money and the earth. I was going to use our soda bottle for a different activity but as I was cutting it up, this project came together perfectly instead. My little preschooler, (Ms. Tiger age 3 at the time) loved painting on the tissue paper. When her rainbow was done she would hold it up by the window and watch the sunlight shine through the colorful paper.

Rainbows are a great way to teach colors without feeling like a formal lesson. While we were crafting we talked about all the different colors that appear in a rainbow and the order in which they appear. After we were done, we pulled out a prism to make rainbows on the wall and chase them around the room.

Step 1. Wash and dry your soda bottle. Cut the top and bottom off so you are left with a tube. Cut the tube in half, to make two

symmetrical arches (1 for each rainbow).

Step 2. Secure the long sides of the arches to a paper plate with tape.

Step 3. Cut the tissue paper into small squares and prepare glue by mixing it with a bit of water to make it easier to brush on.

Step 4. Gently brush glue onto the soda bottle and stick tissue paper on top. I showed Ms. Tiger a picture of a rainbow and let her freely create hers.

Step 5. When you're done decorating your rainbow, glue cotton balls onto the paper plate to make the fluffy clouds.

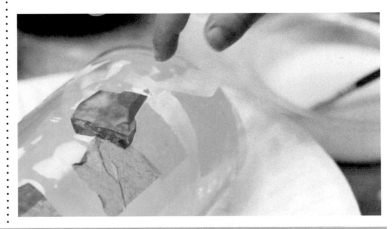

Katie Pinch - A Little Pinch of Perfect

Hi my name is Katie and I'm a busy mommy who can be found covered in paint or running wild in the backyard all to entertain my son and daughter. After studying Recreation Therapy and learning how to develop activities that facilitate learning through play, I became a stay-at-home mom and blogger so I could share all the fun activities we do with other parents looking for inspiration. http://www.alittlepinchofperfect.com/

Engaging Kids In Nature & Outdoors

Sensory, Science

Baby

Toddler

Pre-school

Kinder-garten

How to:

With so much stimulation on screens and with toys, it can sometimes be a challenge to get kids to explore the natural world. We want our kids to love and appreciate nature and the outdoors, but how do we make that happen? Here are a few tips we've used to get our kids engaged in nature and outdoor exploration from their baby days onwards.

Get outside and into nature as often as possible. We live in the middle of a HUGE city, so this can be a challenge. We take walks on our neighborhood green belt, visit the nature preserve, and our local arboretum. If the weather permits we play outside every day. We created a little space in our backyard for a "discovery garden" where the kids collect rocks, sticks, and various treasures to explore.

Talk about what you see, smell, and hear. We smell the flowers. We touch the dirt. We pick up rocks, flowers, and sticks. Talk about all of it with your kids and don't be afraid to let them get their hands dirty. Their natural curiosity will come out and they will wonder about everything they see.

Have the older ones teach the younger ones. Our son loves to show his baby sister all that he knows about the natural world. We go on a "baby school" walk and he shows her the birds, talks about the trees, and picks up flowers, leaves, and sticks to show her. They both love it and are completely engaged with each other and the natural world.

Meet animals face to face. Ideally this would happen in the wild, but that isn't always possible. If you are city locked like we are, this means a visit to the pet store, animal shelter, zoo, or aquarium. Learning about animals in books or on television shows is great, but meeting them up close is so much better. Farm visits can be really fun and allow kids to meet the animals that provide their food.

Visit beautiful places. We try to make sure our family vacations include outdoor exploration. Hiking with kids can be a fun expansion on your neighborhood nature walks and teach your kids so much about the world. Giving your kids a love of the outdoors and adventures in beautiful places can be a fantastic gift. No electronics can compare with a beautiful mountain vista, ocean waves, or natural waterfalls.

The most important thing to remember when trying to engage your kids in nature and the outdoors, is that you have to be engaged with them. Put down the phone and the camera and get down on their level to talk and play and explore. You will create special memories and help develop a love and appreciation of the natural world in your little ones.

Becca Eby - Bare Feet on the Dashboard

Becca is a follower of Jesus, wife, and mother of two precious wee ones. She loves all things crafty and adventurous, and blogs about her frugal family, living debt free, home preschool, travel, homemaking, and parenting at Bare Feet on the Dashboard. http://www.barefeetonthedashboard.com/

Taste Safe Finger Paints

Sensory, Play Recipes, Color Learning

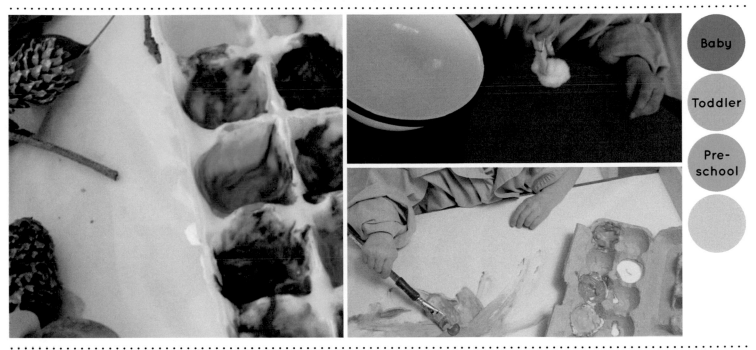

Baby

Toddler

Pre-school

You will need:

Water
Flour
Food coloring
Corn starch
Yogurt
Paper
Splash mat
Paint brushes

How to:

Young babies and children love and appreciate tactile experiences. Store-bought paint is not always safe for babies to play with, so we love making homemade, edible paint — it is the cheapest and safest option for babies and preschoolers alike! There are many easy options using everyday kitchen products, so if your child tries to sneak a taste {and they will!}, you can rest assured. You can present your "paint" in a small, low dish, muffin tin or old egg carton.

Here are a couple ideas for how to safely paint with your baby!

1. Paint with water! Give your child a piece of construction paper, either a large paint brush or a cotton ball on a clothespin, and a small dish of water. They will love the darkened color that forms on their paper! Simple as that.

2. Paint with flour and water! Mix equal parts flour with water, or water colored with food coloring, and mix to the consistency you desire -- try 1/2 cup of each to start. Your child can use their hands or a paint brush and will love the experience!

3. Paint with cornstarch and water! Mix equal parts cornstarch with water, or water colored with food coloring, and mix to your desired consistency. This substance is so fun to work with and the solid-type liquid will amaze both you and your child during painting exploration time!

4. Paint with yogurt! Mix a little food coloring with some plain yogurt.

5. Paint with a heated flour and water recipe! Mix 1/4 cup flour with 1 cup water and heat on a medium stove top until the mixture is smoothed. Use immediately. We pour ours into an egg carton and mix food coloring into each individual section. This recipe takes a little more time, but has a really lovely consistency for either using brushes or little fingers!

There is no need to measure out these recipes -- get them out quickly and watch your little one smile. The painting process is the reason for this experience, not a beautiful product or painting that you will want to share. Your child may dig a giant hole in their paper, and that is okay -- they are discovering textures! Also let your child paint on a splash mat or a sheet, inside a cardboard box, on a piece of mirror or wood, or even in the bathtub! Enjoy your time together.

Amy Smith, M.Ed. - Wildflower Ramblings

Amy Smith, M.Ed., is a kindergarten teacher turned stay at home mom to her two children. She loves Classical, Montessori, and Reggio-inspired learning and teaching. Amy is a Sergeant First Class in the Army Reserve and blogs at Wildflower Ramblings about homeschooling, sensory play, herbal remedies, and their grace filled lives. http://wildflowerramblings.com/

Puppy Dog Paper Tube Craft

Fine Motor, DIY Toys, Imagination Play

Pre-school

Kinder-garten

You will need:

Paper tube
Brown paper
Light brown paper
Googly eyes
Glue
Clear tape
Black marker
Scissors

How to:

Paper tube crafts and activities are a great way for kids to play, craft, and learn. Paper towel tubes, toilet paper tubes, and wrapping paper tubes are abundant and easy to find, and that makes them the perfect material for crafting with kids.

Kids will love to make this puppy dog craft with a few items and a paper tube. This craft can then be used in pretend play activities with kids while exploring language, imagination, storytelling, and songs, all while playing with something that your child created. What a fun way to encourage self-confidence through crafts!

Cut the brown paper to fit your paper tube. You will want to wrap the paper all the way around the paper tube to make the dog's fur. Tape the edges with clear tape. From the dark brown paper, cut two kidney bean-shaped pieces that will become the dog's ears. Cut two "baseball cap" shaped pieces that will become the dog's hind legs, two semi-circles for the front paws, and a tail

all from the dark brown paper. From the light brown paper, cut a small circle that will become the puppy's nose. Older children can cut these pieces on their own. Younger kids can follow directions or copy an example for direction following and sequencing work while creating.

Glue the ear pieces at the top of the tube and the light brown circle on the dog's face. Glue the googly eyes above the circle and add details with the black marker. Glue the tail to the back of the tube and the hind legs and front paws near the base of the cardboard tube. The hind legs will help the tube to stand upright.

Let the glue dry on the puppy craft and then get ready to play!

Encouraging pretend play with crafted materials is a good way to build self-confidence in a child. They can play and pretend with an item that they created! Bring small figures into play scenes with the cardboard tube puppy to reenact stories or conversations. Act out songs such as "How much is that doggie in the window?"

Colleen Beck, OTR/L - Sugar Aunts

Colleen is the owner and chief author of Sugar Aunts, a blog by three sisters who love to share creative activities and crafts. Colleen is a mother to four and an AUNT to eleven nieces and nephews. She is an occupational therapist and loves to pull developmental areas into her posts. Colleen also writes at Mommy Needs a Coffee Break.
http://www.sugaraunts.com/

Balloons and Boxes

Gross Motor, Color Learning

Toddler

Pre-school

Kinder-garten

You will need:

200 water balloons of various colors
One box for each of the colors of water balloons
One kitchen timer (for older children)

How to:

This activity focuses on helping preschoolers sort colors. This is an outside activity that will help them improve their gross motor coordination. This activity works well with small to medium sized groups of children.

Objective 1: To help preschoolers recognize and sort colors.
Objective 2: Improve the gross motor control of preschoolers.

There are two variations for this activity.

Summer variation:
Fill the water balloons with water and place in a container. Place the container in the middle of a field, back yard, or park. Set out boxes labeled with the color the box is supposed to contain, making sure the boxes are 20 or so feet away from the container of balloons.

Winter variation:
Fill the water balloons with air and place in a garbage sack. Place the garbage sack in the middle of a field, back yard, or park. Set out boxes labeled with the color each box is supposed to contain,

making sure the boxes are 20 or so feet away from the container of balloons.

For either variation, tell the children the object of the activity is to get all the balloons sorted into the boxes. The colors need to match; the red balloons go into the box marked red, and so forth. Children should be instructed to only carry one balloon at a time to increase the length of the activity or to avoid children monopolizing the balloons. To mix up the activity, the children can be challenged to sort the balloons in a limited amount of time.

For younger children, ages 2 ½ or 3, don't use a time element. To reinforce color recognition, the children can be challenged to pick up only one color of balloon at a time. After all the balloons are sorted, let the children enjoy free-play time with the balloons.

Deborah - Mommy Crusader and her Knights and Ladies

Deborah's blog is named so because her children are always playing princess and knight, and sometimes being a mommy feels like a crusade. She has five children, 10 and under, and one awesome and supportive husband. With her bachelor's degree in Interpersonal Communication, she writes about parenting tips and fun kid's activities and crafts with a focus on preschool learning activities. http://mommycrusader.com/

FineCraft

Fine Motor, Imagination Play

Pre-school

Kinder-garten

You will need:

Plenty of wine corks or bottle caps (Whole Foods has a wine cork recycling program, they have provided me with wine corks for projects in the past)
Milk Cartons
Lids
Medicine Containers
Stickers
Adhesives (we used an extra-strength, child-safe glue)
Embellishments like glitter, pompoms, etc.
A platform (we used an old Melissa and Doug box, a piece of cardboard works, too)
Creativity and imagination

How to:

My son is obsessed with Minecraft and while I agree that there are many benefits to this game, I hate competing with an electronic device for his attention. One day, I had a very long to-do list and I decided that it was a good time to bring out the electronic device. We were driving around in the car all day and I was grateful that Minecraft helped distract my boy while we ran our errands. The problem with Minecraft is that he can never get enough playing time. He would be perfectly content playing all day long and he surely was not going to stop without a complaint.

As soon as we got home, I got busy with dinner prep. Of course, my boy saw this as an opportunity to ask for more Minecraft time but I felt that he'd already had plenty of screen time and

there were many other options for him to choose from now that we were back home. He pouted of course and said he was "bored to death." I let him sit in deadly boredom for just a little bit to prove to him that boredom won't kill him but as I was cooking I remembered that I'd been collecting random items (wine corks, spice containers, lids etc....) meant for a project yet to be determined.

I put them all in a box and gave them to my son along with adhesives, stickers, and other embellishments. I told him that he was free to use the material in any way he chose. He sat at the kitchen table for a few minutes taking stock of his inventory and before long he began building his masterpiece which he aptly named his "WineCraft FineCraft". It looked so fun that my husband and I joined in on the design and creating our WineCraft FineCraft construction became a fun bonding activity for the three of us.

This type of open ended craft project builds critical thinking skills, spatial awareness, creativity and fine motor skills all while the children are having fun!

Shelah - Mosswood Connections

Shelah Moss is an autism consultant, tutor and mother. Her goal in life is to continue to learn and teach while having fun. http://mosswoodconnections.com/

Process Art & Children's Development

Fine Motor, Color Learning

Toddler

Pre-school

Kinder-garten

You will need:

Tray or shallow box
One color of a variety of drawing materials (crayons, markers, colored pencils, pens, highlighters)
Paper

How to:

What is Process Art?
Process art is an experience that focuses on the making of the artwork rather than on the end product. There are no step-by-step directions or right and wrong way for a child to create their art. Each artwork is unique and original to each child.

Why is Process Art important?
Children learn through playing, asking questions and being allowed to explore their world or environment. This freedom of expression and opportunity to make their own choices helps develop their creative and critical thinking skills.

What does Process Art look like?
Painting with colors and different size brushes.
Exploring and building with clay or play dough.
Painting or stamping with unusual materials (like paint rollers, kitchen utensils or vegetables.)
Making collages with different types of tape, and colored and patterned papers.

Tips for creating Process Art with children:
Arrange materials in an inviting way, creating an open invitation to explore and create with the materials. Let the child have time to experiment with the tools and materials. Play music in the background.

Create a Process Art Invitation to Explore One Color
Step 1: Arrange the materials in an inviting way.

Step 2: Allow your child time to explore and create with the materials. Remember there is no wrong way to create the artwork.

Step 3: Ask open ended questions along the way such as, "Tell me about your picture." By asking your child questions this helps promote creative thinking and stretches their thinking.

Step 4: Hang and display. Allow your child to select an artwork to hang up and display. This gives them a sense of accomplishment and self pride.

There are many possibilities on how to create open invitations to create process art. This activity has a few suggestions to help get you started.

Jamie Hand - Hand Made Kids Art

HandMade**KIDSArt**

Jamie is a certified Art Instructor having taught children of all ages. In addition to inspiring young minds and creating for Hand Made Kids Art, she is a busy mom of 3 children. Hand Made Kids Art focuses on quick, easy and inspiring art activities to grow creative kids. It doesn't matter if you only have 5 minutes or 20 minutes, you can find time to create art with your children with Hand Made Kids Art. http://handmadekidsart.com/

Take Flight with Digital Photography

Imagination Play

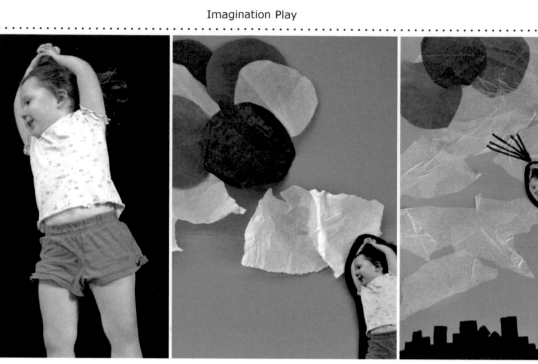

Pre-school

Kinder-garten

You will need:

Construction paper
Tissue paper
Digital camera or cell phone camera
Printer
Glue
Foam brush
Black permanent marker

How to:

Take flight in a mixed media work of art that combines collage and digital photography. Brainstorm with your child different ways a person can take flight. You may discuss ideas such as an airplane, hot air balloon, or space rocket. Let your child be creative even if it is not a realistic solution. Choose one method of flight to re-create into a work of art.

Step 1. After discussing with your child how to visually represent their idea of flight, have the child lay on the floor and strike a pose to best show their idea. Let them try several different poses if needed to experiment what pose works best for their idea. Remember, let your child lead the project.

Step 2. Take a photo of your child laying on the floor with their selected pose. Print out the photograph. Design Tip: Have your child lay down on a dark solid color blanket or bedsheet to make it easier to cut out later.

Step 3. Have the child cut out their image from the photograph. Use tissue paper or construction paper to cut additional shapes to help tell the visual story of taking flight. Design Tip: Layout your collage pieces before gluing.

Step 4. Glue your photo and paper collage pieces to create the collage. Let the glue dry.

Step 5. Once the paper is completely dry, use a black permanent marker to add drawing details to help tell the visual story. Hang artwork and display.

Jamie Hand - Hand Made Kids Art

Jamie is a certified Art Instructor having taught children of all ages. In addition to inspiring young minds and creating for Hand Made Kids Art, she is a busy mom of 3 children. Hand Made Kids Art focuses on quick, easy and inspiring art activities to grow creative kids. It doesn't matter if you only have 5 minutes or 20 minutes, you can find time to create art with your children with Hand Made Kids Art. http://handmadekidsart.com/

Frozen Winter Sensory Bin

Pre-school

Kinder-garten

You will need:

2 cups White Pearl Barley
1 container
Blue food colouring
1 Plastic zipped bag
Measuring cups, spoons
Silver Christmas decoration

How to:

I am sure you have heard of the movie Frozen. My preschooler is a little obsessed with the movie and I decided to follow her lead and create a Frozen-inspired sensory bin.

I have a love-hate relationship with our preschool sensory activities, in particular sensory bins. I love the joy and fun that my kids have with it but I hate the clean up and the mess. I am very happy for my vacuum and keep it handy. Before attempting this bin, ensure that you have a vacuum nearby for quick clean up. You have been warned.

Place 1 cup of the barley in the plastic zipped bag and add 10 drops of food colouring as well as 1 teaspoon water. Shake vigourously in order to distribute the food colouring evenly. Leave plastic zipped bag overnight to dry.

Add the colored barley, plain barley and silver decorations to the container. Next, place a measuring cup, measuring spoon and anything else you think your preschooler will love to play with.

Once I gave my daughter the go ahead, she ran happily to her bin. She practiced her pouring and scooping skills by using her measuring cup and spoon. She also practiced counting- she counted each scoop of barley she poured into her cup. I even overheard her talking to her little brother and telling him this is her sensory bin and that he can play with it. I even got invited to play with her. There is something about hearing my daughter say the words, "Mommy play with me please?" that melts my heart.

J played with her bin for almost 2 hours and once again we had to negotiate with her and tell her she could play with it tomorrow. If you like this sensory activity, be sure to check out my Facebook Page where I share several activities as well as my Pinterest board for more inspiration.

Alecia Francois - Learning 2 Walk

Alecia is a preschool blogger at Learning 2 Walk where she shares preschool resources such as sensory activities and letter worksheets for homeschooling moms. When she is not blogging, she is busily keeping her 2 children J (her headstrong preschooler) and C (her destructive cuddle bug) safe. http://learning2walk.com/

Discovery Bags for Babies

Sensory

Baby

You will need:

Food Storage Bag (Gallon-size plastic zipped bags)
Material to fill bag: Hair gel, water beads, jello, or water & oil.

How to:

Creating a sensory activity for babies can be difficult, since they tend to put everything in their mouth! One way to create a sensory experience for them is by creating discovery bags. Discovery bags are wonderful for children to use their sense of touch and sight to explore. To make a discovery bag, you will need a strong food storage bag and items to fill it. The bag must be strong enough to withstand handling by a child, so make sure it is sturdy or place one bag inside of another bag. You can also add extra tape to all 4 sides to make it secure.

Here are 4 ideas for filling discovery bags:

1. Hair Gel - Scoop hair gel into the bag. Add in colorful items, such as buttons, sequins, glitter, beads, and more. Try to stay away from objects that could poke a hole in the bag.

2. Water Beads - Simply add water beads to a bag. Since water beads are a choking hazard to babies, it works well to seal them in a bag so babies can still feel the squishy beads without actually touching them. You can find water beads in the floral section of craft stores.

3. Oil & Water - Pour oil into a bag. Drop in food coloring. Then pour a little water into the bag. Close the bag and watch how it creates color blobs and bubbles. When you poke the color blobs with your finger, they break off and create more.

4. Jello - Make jello and add it to the bag. Include other items in the bag for your little one to look at.

After you create the discovery bags, invite your little one to explore them. I suggest taping the bag down to the table or floor where you play. Another idea is to tape the bag to the window and watch the sun shine through them. While all the ingredients are contained in the bag, please make sure the bag is always secure and you are supervising your baby.

Discovery bags are a great way for babies to play and discover new things about the world they live in!

Angela Thayer - Teaching Mama

Angela is a wife to an amazing man. mama to three boys, lover of the Midwest, and daughter of Christ. She loves to create hands-on learning activities for her little ones and shares them on her blog, Teaching Mama.
http://teachingmama.org/

Teaching Mama
playing, creating, and learning at home

Peppermint-Scented Slime Play

Sensory, Play Recipes

Pre-school

Kinder-garten

You will need:

1/2 cup school glue + 1 extra tablespoon (a little less than one 4 oz. bottle)
1/2 cup liquid starch (sold in laundry aisle)
1/2 teaspoon peppermint extract
10-15 drops green food coloring (depends on how dark you want it to be)
1-2 tablespoons green craft glitter (optional)

How to:

Slime is a fun, unique sensory play material perfect for curious preschoolers. This peppermint-scented sparkle slime is a variation of the classic jelly slime. It will instantly fill your kitchen with a refreshing minty smell and provide your child a chance to play and explore through the sense of touch, sight, and smell!

Recipe:
Step 1. In medium-sized bowl, mix 1/2 cup + 1 extra tablespoon school glue, 1/2 teaspoon peppermint extract, and 10-15 drops green food coloring. If you want to add sparkles, mix those in now as well. (Sparkles will get on hands and the play surface when you play with this slime, but easily wipe off when playtime is over.) Make sure everything is thoroughly mixed before moving onto Step 2. The peppermint scent should smell amazing!

Step 2. Give your liquid starch bottle a few shakes to make sure it's well-mixed. Then stir the liquid starch into your green peppermint glue mixture 1 tablespoon at a time, MIXING THOROUGHLY with each tablespoon, until it takes on the form of slime. A good slime should be squishy but not sticky.

Step 3. Mix and squeeze your slime mixture for several minutes. If your slime doesn't mold together and is stringy after 5-10 minutes of mixing and kneading, DON'T PANIC! Do some simple troubleshooting. If it's stringy and slippery, add a little bit of glue. If it's stringy and sticky, add a little bit of liquid starch. If it's too watery, pour some of the liquid out and let the mixture sit in an airtight container for an hour or so to absorb the extra moisture.

Time to play! You can smash, stretch, poke holes, pound, snip with scissors, build shapes and letters, or even practice cutting with a fork and knife. For hesitant kids, let them touch with tools first instead of fingers. Great way to ease in and still have fun!

Be sure to wash hands after playing with slime. If it gets on clothes, toss them in the wash and it should come right out. Store slime in an airtight container and it should stay good for at least a few weeks. Inspect prior to each play session to make sure it's still good. This slime recipe is only appropriate for children who will not put their hands in their mouth or eyes during play.

Christie Kiley - Mama OT

Christie is a mom and pediatric occupational therapist who loves to have fun while helping children reach their potential. She blogs at MamaOT.com she shares tips, tricks, and information to encourage, educate, and empower those who care for children. http://MamaOT.com/

Craft Stick Color Sorting

Fine Motor, DIY Toys, Color Learning

Pre-school

You will need:

Colored craft sticks (can usually find at the dollar store)
Empty coffee can with plastic lid (slightly taller than craft sticks)
Permanent markers in colors that match the craft sticks
Sharp knife or scissors (keep away from children!)

How to:

This simple preschool activity challenges a variety of developmental skills such as grasp patterns, hand-eye coordination, bilateral coordination (coordinating the use of both hands), in-hand manipulation (moving and adjusting items using only one hand), working at and reaching across the middle of the body, visual discrimination (finding the colors you need amidst visual distractions), color matching, and concentration.

Step 1. Gather your colored craft sticks and cut slits in the lid of an empty coffee can. The number of slits should correspond to the number of stick colors. Slits should be wide enough for the sticks to fit in, yet thin enough that they provide a bit of resistance so the child will have to use his or her finger muscles to push the sticks down into the can.

Step 2. Once your slits are just the right size, use permanent markers to thickly outline the slits to match the colors of craft sticks you have. If you only have neutral-colored craft sticks, just color the ends of the sticks with your permanent markers so they can still be used for matching colors.

That's it, time to play! You can set the materials out as an invitation to play, or you can engage in this activity right alongside your child. It's a completely flexible activity depending on your child's skill and interest level.

You can show your preschooler how to match and push the colors in but, really, they may be able to figure out how to do it on their own if they are already familiar with the concept of matching colors. If they do figure it out on their own (or with just a little bit of guidance), then that means this is a just-right challenge for them! If it appears the concept of matching colors goes over their head, then it probably means they aren't quite ready for it, and that's okay. Stick with non-color coded slits for now, let your little one problem solve how to pinch and push the sticks into the can, and come back to the color-matching concept in a little while. Pay attention to whether the slits provide too much resistance and adjust accordingly to promote a balance of challenge and success.

Once all the craft sticks have been pushed into the container, your child can use their strength and coordination to open, dump, and repeat!

Christie Kiley - Mama OT

Christie is a mom and pediatric occupational therapist who loves to have fun while helping children reach their potential. She blogs at MamaOT.com she shares tips, tricks, and information to encourage, educate, and empower those who care for children. http://MamaOT.com/

Recycled Water Bottle Fish

Fine Motor, DIY Toys

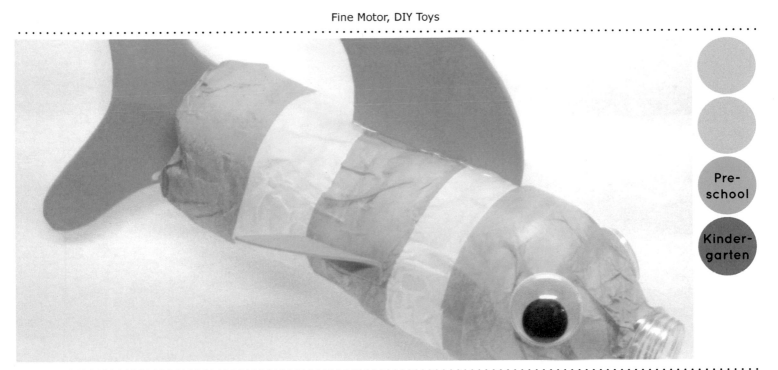

Pre-school

Kinder-garten

You will need:

Clean and dry water bottle, with wrapper and plastic cap removed
Brightly colored tissue paper (Leftovers from gifts work great!)
Craft foam
Googly eyes
White craft glue and an old paint brush
Hot glue gun and glue sticks

How to:

Recyclables are a cheap and wonderful crafting material, and water bottles are one of our favorites when it comes to getting creative. This craft uses both recycled water bottles and tissue paper left over from birthday gifts to create colorful, one-of-a-kind fish!

To begin crafting our fish, I had the kids rip up squares of brightly colored tissue paper. This is a great activity for building hand strength for later writing skills.

While the squares are great for giving the fish a multi-colored collage look, we also cut 1-inch thick strips of tissue paper, which are perfect if you want a striped fish instead.

Once the tissue paper was ready, I had each of them use an old paint brush to paint white craft glue on the outside of their water bottle. It helps to only use a little glue at a time, adding pieces of tissue paper as you go, instead of covering the whole bottle with glue at once. Also, you may want to have a damp paper towel handy for wiping excess glue off so the tissue paper doesn't keep getting stuck to little fingers.

Once the water bottle was covered in tissue paper, we let the whole thing dry (about an hour).

Then it was time to use the craft foam to create our fish's fins. For younger children you may want to cut out the pieces yourself. For older children, you could draw the design on the craft foam and have them cut it out, or let them design the fins completely on their own.

We used a hot glue gun to add googly eyes and the craft foam fins and tail to our fish. Please remember, hot glue can get extremely hot! This is a step best suited for an adult to do. Young children can easily point out where each piece should go while the adult works the hot glue gun.

The best part of using hot glue is that your one-of-a-kind creation will be ready to play with, or display, as soon as the glue cools.

These brightly colored fish look beautiful hanging from the ceiling in our play area!

Christina Schul - There's Just One Mommy

Christina is the author of There's Just One Mommy, where she shares learning activities and craft ideas for children. She has a Master's degree in education and spent 11 years in the classroom before becoming a stay-at-home mom to her two children, whom she now homeschools. http://theresjustonemommy.com/

Fun Activities To Enjoy Works Of Art

Imagination Play

Pre-school

Kinder-garten

How to:

Your kids are not too young to enjoy looking at art! Looking at art opens kids up to new cultures and ideas, helps them learn empathy, and develops creativity and critical thinking skills. Try some of these activities out with your little one in front of any artwork of your choosing to get her engaged with works of art.

1. Talk about it. This can be as simple as pointing out funny things, counting objects, or discussing shapes.
2. Move! Put your bodies into the position of the characters, pantomime the actions, make up a dance, or play charades.
3. Play "I spy." One person chooses something from the artwork and gives hints about it while the other people guess what it is.
4. Make a texture bag. Place a textured object that is similar to something in the artwork in a bag. Have the child reach into the bag, feel the texture, and describe it without looking at it.
5. Make up a story about the artwork together. What happened before the scene in the art? What will happen next?
6. Integrate your child's toys. Use the artwork as the spark for some pretend play. Use blocks to build the scene or use toy characters to act out the story. Take the child's lead.
7. Draw the artwork. Drawing the artwork makes the child spend more time looking at it. The more looking they do, the more they benefit from the experience.
8. Practice description skills. Have the child describe the artwork to someone who has never seen it before. If old enough, have the second person draw the artwork based on the description of the child.
9. Visit an art museum and play. Did you know that most art museums offer special materials for families to use in the galleries? Ask at the front desk if they have any family guides or resources to use on your visit. These often include scavenger hunts, discussion guides, games, and/or books to read in front of artworks.
10. Have a museum scavenger hunt. Before you go, print a small clip from the artwork or a picture of an item from the artwork. (Check out the museum's website to find out what is on view). Then, have the kids look for their picture in the museum.

Try it out, don't stress, and have fun!

the Art Curator for Kids

Cindy Ingram - The Art Curator for Kids

Cindy Ingram was once an art teacher and museum educator with an MA in Art Education, and is now a work-at-home mom of two lovely daughters (ages 3 and 5). She is passionate about the power of art in people's lives and writes about how to teach art appreciation and enjoy art history with kids of all ages at The Art Curator for Kids. http://artcuratorforkids.com/

Drawing Around Household Items

Imagination Play, Shapes, Life Skills

You will need:

Pick random things around the house without too much plan-ning: keys, CD, pen, spaghetti, LEGOs, cloth and paper pins, orange peel.
White paper
Pen or crayons

How to:

Let your child pick one of the random items you picked around the house and tell them that the item is part of the drawing. Place it on the paper and let the drawing begin. Enjoy the process of this simple art.

Try to stay away from giving ideas of what the drawing should be after you put the random item on the paper. Let the child use his/her pure and brilliant imagination, and, believe me, you won't be sorry.

If the child is having hard time deciding what to draw with a particular item, engage into conversations about the item's shape and where do we see this shape. Talk more about the item itself and how is it used. Eventually, the child will come up with an idea that will blow your mind.

Why Is This Art Activity So Brilliant And So Beneficial For Your Child?
We had a chance to talk about the shapes of those random items. We compared them and tried to relate to real objects. The imagination is being used over the roof during this art activity.

It's amazing how children can have such adaptive minds.

My daughter was amazed about how such a simple item like an orange peel could contribute to her drawing. She started seeing the possibilities of art in a totally different level. We agreed that anything could be art and it doesn't have to be done with expensive art supplies.

I think this art activity is perfect for beginner drawers. The items help them stay in the proportions of the future drawing and keeps on track with an idea. That's why, in my opinion, my daughter's drawings came out so good.

It was such a great imagination game and an awesome art activity. I strongly recommend you try it with your kids. It's simple, free, educational and super fun!

P·L·A·Y tivities

Birute Efe - Playtivities

Birute has daily fun at her Playtivities.com blog and the farm where she lives with her family. She loves creating activities and toys for her 2 kiddos by up-cycling household items. She will never pass by a big cardboard box or a pile of old magazines. She believes the best learning comes from exploring and creating.
http://playtivities.com

Sparkly-Shiny-Jingly Wind Ornaments

Fine Motor

Pre-school

Kinder-garten

You will need:

Small plastic embroidery hoop
Approximately 12 yards of medium-width ribbon
Approximately 6 yards of thin ribbon
Small jingle bells
Small metallic beads

How to:

My little girls love looking out of our windows and seeing anything colorful, swirly, or sparkly. We've got pinwheels, wind chimes, birdfeeders and wind socks that they 'ooh' and 'ahh' over. These beautiful ribbon wind ornaments have certainly added some sparkly flare to our yard since we made them, and they'll make a nice addition to your yard as well. They look so pretty blowing in the breeze and make the loveliest soft little jingling sound. On top of all that, making them is great project to help develop your child's fine motor skills. Here's how to make some for your own yard.

Gather your materials. Start by cutting the thicker ribbons into lengths of about 24 inches (60 cm). You do want some variation in the length to make the project look more fluid. Next, cut thin ribbons to be a little bit longer than the thick ribbons. You need some extra length to accommodate several knots that you'll be tying. Be sure to cut the ribbons at a sharp angle to reduce fraying.

Tie your ribbons all along the embroidery hoop using two simple overhand knots. You can make a pattern if you like, but I think

it looks just as nice to have some variety. Most preschoolers can learn how to tie a simple knot, so this is great fine motor work for them. On the thin ribbons, add the sparkly beads and jingle bells. Thread a bead or jingle bell, then tie some small knots right below where you want it to sit on the ribbon, to keep it from sliding down. Again, letting your child thread the beads and jingle bells is great for fine motor development. We added about 2 beads and 2 jingle bells to each thin ribbon.

To tie the ribbons from which you'll hang your wind ornament, simply tie three longer ribbons, evenly spaced around your circle and gather them on top and tie them together.

You can then tie a loop and hang your ornament from a hook on your porch, a tree branch, or a free standing shepherd's hook. Now sit back, relax, and watch it fly in the breeze!

Ellen - Cutting Tiny Bites

Ellen is a former teacher who now channels all that energy into staying at home with her two young daughters. She writes at CuttingTinyBites.com about crafting, early learning, homeschool preschool, parenting ideas, and vegetarian cooking. http://www.cuttingtinybites.com/

Make Your Own Log Catapult

Fine Motor, DIY Toys, Science

Kinder-garten

You will need:

8 logs with two slots
5 2" rubber bands
1 3" strong rubber band
1 bottle cap
1 piece of masking tape
Ammunition (small balls)

How to:

One day, when my son and my husband were setting up one of their elaborate wooden log scenes, they decided they needed some catapults so they could shoot at each other's forts.

They set out to build one out of toy logs. It turned out great and was a lot of fun to play with. I just love activities that get my son learning, as well as playing and having a great time.

Give this awesome DIY Log Catapult a try. I'm sure your kids will get a lot of satisfaction out of building their own toy. Enjoy!

Image 1: Logs needed and sizes of rubber bands.

Image 2: Create a box with 4 logs. Add strong 3 inch rubber band to the back log.

Image 3: Note: The front of the catapult does not have a rubber band on it.

Add 2 logs to the sides, going from front to back. Add 1 more log to the front going from side to side.

Image 4: Check image 4 to make sure it matches the image. Once you start adding the rubber bands, always make sure they are in the grooves.
To add the catapult arm piece, loop the (red) rubber band around the top front log and slip the catapult arm log into the rubber band loop.

Image 5: Secure the 4 ends of your build by double looping rubber bands over the corners where the logs intersect. Stretch the strong (blue) rubber band toward the front and slip it between the two front horizontal logs. This is a little tricky to do. Once you slip it in between the logs, stretch it up over the bottom of the catapult arm log.

Image 6: Take a soda bottle cap and attach it to the arm with masking tape.

Image 7: Load your catapult bucket with ammunition, pull back and FIRE!

Most of the time we shoot little plastic balls and small logs. You can also use wadded up paper, aluminum foil balls, pom poms etc. (The balls shown are from our Playmobil sets.)

I hope you and your kids enjoy trying out this Make Your Own Log Catapult project and that you experiment and design one of your own as well. This is a fun activity that is packed with learning opportunities.

Sheila Rogers - Brain Power Boy

Sheila is the publisher of Brain Power Boy, a website that focuses on raising boys who love to learn. Her passion for helping parents find great resources for boys comes through in her posts on activities for boys, LEGO, homeschool unit studies, learning styles, the best books for boys and more. http://brainpowerboy.com/

Monster Wooden Blocks

DIY Toys

Toddler

Pre-school

Kinder-garten

You will need:

A set of wooden building blocks
Non-toxic paints (like acrylic paints in our case)
A black marker
A varnish that will work with the paint you use (like glossy acrylic varnish in our case)

How to:

Wooden building blocks are a classic toy for open-ended play. Stacking and organizing them aids in the development of dexterity, hand-eye coordination and in imagining forms in three dimensions. So, you cannot be blamed for picking up another set for your kids whenever you see a good deal at a second-hand toy store or dollar store. If you have a pretty good assortment already, or some that are starting to need a makeover, you might consider turning a batch of wooden blocks into MONSTER BLOCKS!

Unpack your blocks. Children's blocks don't usually require any preparatory sanding before painting, which is one of the reasons they are so well suited to this sort of project.

Divide your blocks into groups, and paint each group a different bright colour. We used acrylics for painting, but tempera or gouache would work as well, or you can also try staining them with liquid watercolours.

The fun part! Paint facial features on the blocks and outline them with a fine black marker. Little blocks like cubes and cylinders are good for painting eyes, and long cuboids are great for mouths and moustaches. Add horns, beards and hats! Different sides of one block can have different designs painted onto them. If you have a child who is old enough to help, all the better: turning wooden blocks into monsters can become a family craft!

Once all the layers of paint have thoroughly dried, seal the blocks with a layer of the appropriate varnish. Let the varnish dry, and they are ready to be played with.

Our son was instantly engaged by his monster blocks. First, he giggled himself silly when we built funny faces for him, then went to work on his own creations. There was one thing he had to set straight from the beginning, though - monsters that were caught frowning would be taken apart and rebuilt with a smile! In no time, all of his other building toys were adorned with smiling monster faces, too. He stacked them on top of the LEGO cars and brought some of his Magnatiles over. The blocks have also featured in sorting games - by colour, by shape and by body part. It turns out that open-ended play isn't limited to plain building blocks.

Liska Myers - Adventure in a Box

When not building towers and measuring the depth of puddles with her toddler, Liska likes to make toys and write about them. She is also a bookworm and fond of painting. Accompanied by her husband and son, she lives and adventures in Ontario, Canada. http://adventure-in-a-box.com/

Magical Mini Worlds

Imagination Play

Toddler

Pre-school

Kinder-garten

You will need:

Potting mix: purchase high quality potting mix and always use gloves when handling

Plants: herbs, grasses, flowering annuals and hardy succulents all work well

Small, plastic figurines: dinosaurs, fairies, farm animals, wild animals, elves, insects, vehicles, the choice is yours (or at least your child's!)

Rocks

Coloured, glass fairy stones

Seashells

Sticks: these can be bundled or glued together to form simple structures, bridges or fences

Pieces of tree bark

Interesting seedpods

Large buttons or plastic lids: can be used as colourful stepping stones

A small, upturned plastic plant pot or washed butter container: can serve as a shelter with a simple door and window cut out with a utility knife

An upturned shell, foil pie tray or shallow bowl can act as a pool or pond

Pre-loved CDs and oversized sequins can provide a hint of magical sparkle

Fill your container with potting mix and plant your choice of plants, watering well.

Then it's time for the fun to really begin! Put on your treasure-hunting hat and gather any of the above things.

A visit to your local discount store, hardware or garden nursery can provide further inspiration for your mini world. Look for small-scale items like bird houses, brightly coloured pinwheels and other garden figurines.

How to:

Some children love being outdoors. Others need gentle encouragement to discover the wonders of the natural world and the joy of playing outdoors. One way of providing this encouragement is to capture their imagination by involving them in creating a magical mini world.

A garden for fairies, an oasis for safari animals, a wetland for frogs and lizards, an island for dinosaurs – your magical mini world is limited only by your own imagination. A good place to start your planning is to consider what your child is most interested in, what do they most enjoy playing with? Whether the answer is birds or bulldozers, a mini world can provide a safe, playful space to connect your child with the natural environment.

Mini worlds are a perfect way to encourage children outside into the fresh air. And you never know, encouraging their imaginative play on this small scale may just lead them down the garden path to find and explore more playful opportunities outdoors!

childhood 101
PLAYING | LEARNING | GROWING

Christie Burnett - Childhood 101

Christie Burnett is the mum of two, early childhood teacher, author and blogger. She is passionate about children's play, creativity and learning, and tries hard to prioritise time for family in the busyness of every day life. At Childhood101.com you'll find playful activity and project ideas for kids, family friendly recipes, ideas for family fun and positive parenting reflections. http://childhood101.com/

Experimenting with Watercolours

Fine Motor, DIY Toys, Color Learning

Pre-school

You will need:

Toilet paper & rolls
Liquid watercolours
Paintbrush or dropper (optional)

How to:

Have you ever thought about painting toilet paper? I hadn't either, until my four year old daughter JJ asked if she could try it one day. And I thought, well, why not?

Painting with watercolours on toilet paper is very different to painting on normal paper. Because of it's delicate texture, painting on toilet paper creates the opportunity to study absorbency, as tiny droplets of watercolour bleed out into a much larger surface area. Primary colours can also bleed into each other to create secondary colours, or you can just have fun and see what patterns you can make.

It also provides the opportunity for kids to self-moderate. Don't add too much liquid or the paper will disintegrate. Don't be too rough or the paper will tear.

Kids could paint with droppers (pipettes), their finger, or dab very lightly with a paintbrush as JJ is doing here. She found this process mesmerising, carefully and methodically dabbing around each square, watching the colour bleed, making sure that no white sections remained.

It was JJ who had the great idea to gently wrap the painted squares (whilst still wet) around empty toilet paper rolls. She left an inch or so at the top, so that it looked like a doll wearing a dress. This is very delicate work - great for fine motor skills. The 'dress' stuck to the roll as it dried - no glue required!

Once dried, you could add extra details with a permanent marker if you wish, but my daughter was happy to play with hers just as they were. Apparently her new TP roll dolls were Disney princesses, who fortunately can be distinguished by dress colour alone.

Danya - Danya Banya

Danya is a fun Australian mum to two little girls. She's given up the corporate life to spend her days finger painting, making play dough and creating with toilet paper rolls. She shares ways to play and create with kids on her blog Danya Banya. http://www.danyabanya.com/

Fizzing Hearts

Fine Motor, Science, Science Experiments

Toddler

Pre-school

You will need:

Some paper
White school glue
Baking soda
Vinegar and container to put it in (we used a small glass jar)
Red food coloring (liquid ones)
Fine motor dropper

How to:

Use a fine motor set dropper and make a rather cool Science experiment!

On your paper make the shape of the hearts in glue and sprinkle well with baking soda. I do those on a tray so that I can tap off the loose baking soda and reuse it. Optionally, leave it to dry for 2 hours.

While you can use it just like this I found the almost dry hearts produced more fizz because of the more solid state.

Add a few drops of red food coloring to your vinegar. I just kind of eye balled this one. I must have used 5-10 drops.

Set up your activity on a tray to contain over flow, this is food coloring and vinegar, which we use to dye color rice with! Even add some newspaper if you are rather concerned.

Add the vinegar to the center of the heart and watch it fizz!

My preschooler also discovered that with this dropper it sucked up the vinegar slowly if he pressed gently on the bulb. This provided some more understanding of how this item sucks up the liquid as he could see it going up the twisty part slowly. Almost as much fun as making those hearts fizz!

Nicolette Roux - Powerful Mothering

Hi I'm Nicolette, a SAHM to 4 little ones age 5 and under. I love to share my simple and easy crafts & activities, printables and learning ideas for 0-5 year olds! Author of: Rice Play and 99 Fine Motor ideas for Ages 1-5.
http://www.powerfulmothering.com/

"Children learn as they play. Most importantly, in play children learn how to learn".

- O. Fred Donaldson

Early Childhood Education

Techniques Encouraging Story Writing

Literacy, Writing

STORY WRITING PROMPT

People
Mum
Me
Lily
Zach
Mae
Daddy
Doodles

Beginning
Once upon a time...
There was a boy/girl called...
One night Millie was...
This story is about...
One day I ...

Places
At home
Seaside
Garden
Shops
Work
Playground
Zoo

Middle
"person" went to "place"
When they got there "this" happened
They did..."something"
It was...
They were with...
They were happy/sad...

End
Finally "this" happened
Then they went to...
Everyone was happy
They all lived happily ever after
...went to bed
...went home

Kindergarten

Printable

How to:

A lack of confidence in children can be the root of many issues throughout their education. My six-year-old daughter was recently brought to tears at school during an afternoon literacy lesson.

The class had been asked to write a story and my daughter – who has always struggled with low self-confidence at school –immediately panicked. She didn't believe she could have any "good" ideas and got herself so worked up that her mind went completely blank.

In order to help her gain confidence in writing, we tried out various different story writing methods together at home.

Story prompt – the first idea we came up with was to provide her with a writing prompt. We made a laminated version of this, which she could carry with her. It breaks the story down into its individual parts:

a) Who is in it?
b) Where does it happen?
c) How does it start?
d) What happens in the middle?
e) How does it end?

It also includes some suggestions for each section to give her some inspiration.

Story bag – fill a drawstring bag with a few different items – toys, photos, word prompts, trinkets, any other small accessories such as shells/glove/marble. Ask your child to reach their hand into the bag – without peeking - then root around to select three or more items. Use these items as the basis of the story. For example: photo of the beach, toy dog, LEGO brick, ribbon. These items could encourage them to write a story set at the seaside about a dog and so on.

Complete the story - give them an excerpt from the beginning of a story and ask them to write the middle and ending. Here are some examples:

a) Jimmy loved going to the zoo. He particularly enjoyed watching the penguins swimming around in their pool. One day...

b) Cherry Pickles loved to travel. Her dream was to travel the world in a hot air balloon...

c) There was a storm brewing in the east. The thunderclouds were gathering and heading towards the beach where Charlie was playing with his dog. They ran home just as the rain began, but when they got there...

Sometimes we forget that children need help with their education outside of the classroom as well as with building confidence. Support and encouragement can be easily given, if and when they require it.

Mummy Kettle - 101 things to do with kids

I am a mother to two little monsters - aged 4 and 7. I began blogging in April 2014 and absolutely love doing it! It has encouraged me to spend more quality time with my family, and in particular my children, doing lots of activities I probably would never have dreamed of before. Life is never dull for the Kettles!
http://www.101thingstodowithkids.com/

Wild "Hair" Creatures

Fine Motor, Science

Pre-school

Kinder-garten

You will need:

Small disposable cup
Dirt (enough to fill the cup)
Grass seeds (or substitute with chia seeds)
Items to decorate your cup, such as googly eyes, buttons, pom poms, etc.
Glue to adhere your decorations
Water

How to:

Have you ever grown a Chia Head or Chia Pet? They were quite popular when I was younger, although I never grew one myself. Nonetheless, they were the inspiration behind our decision to create our own creatures with live and growing grass "hair."

This activity touches on a number of curricular areas for young children, including:
- Science (Botany): children will plant seeds and observe them sprout
- Art and creativity: children will create their own grass "hair" creatures
- Fine motor skills: children will improve their scissors skills as they give their creatures "haircuts"

My kids loved creating their own creatures with grass "hair" and giving them "haircuts." And as a parent and educator, I loved that this activity taught them a little bit about how seeds grow. It also taught them patience, since my kids had to wait several days before their creatures were ready for a "haircut."

Step 1 - Select a cup and decorate it however you wish. Turn it into a person, an animal, or simply create some abstract art.
Step 2 - Fill your cup with dirt.
Step 3 - Add a generous heaping of seeds on top of the dirt. Spread them around so they cover the entire surface of the dirt.
Step 4 - Water your seeds, taking care not to add too much.
Step 5 - Set your cup in a sunny location. Continue to monitor the water level and add more water as needed. It won't be long before your seeds begin to sprout!
Step 6 - When your creature's hair is grown, it's haircut time! Give your child a pair of kid-friendly scissors. Then let your child channel her inner hair stylist to give her creature an amazing haircut! (You may want to place a tray or mat underneath to contain the mess.)

If you continue to water and care for your creature after its haircut, the grass will grow back quickly. This will give your child many more opportunities to cut the creature's hair.

Note: I was careful to explain to my children that it was okay for them to give "haircuts" to their creatures, but it was not okay for them to cut their own hair or the hair of other people.

Katie S-G - Gift of Curiosity

Katie is the creative force behind Gift of Curiosity, a resource site for parents, teachers, and caregivers who want to engage children in hands-on, developmentally appropriate educational activities. Katie has a master's degree in education and a Ph.D. in child development. She is also the mom of two curious kids, who provide inspiration for most of the ideas she shares. http://www.giftofcuriosity.com/

Gift of CURIOSITY
Sparking children's creativity and learning

DIY Math Peg Board Game

Fine Motor, DIY Toys, Color Learning, Math, Counting

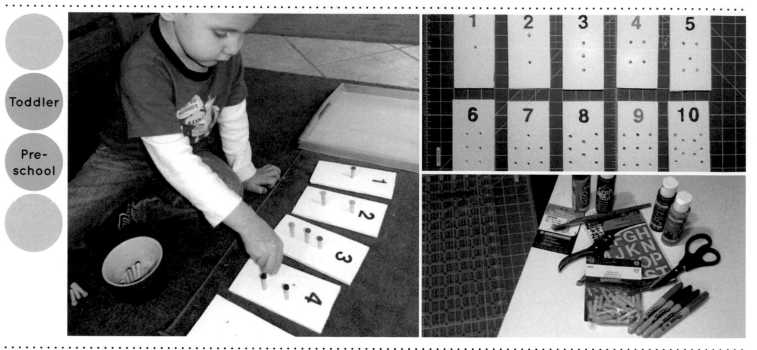

Toddler

Pre-school

You will need:

A piece of foam board
Number stencils
Small wooden pegs
Several colors of paint
Paint brush
Permanent markers
Cutting boards
Rotary cutter
Needle nose pliers

How to:

I looked up buying a peg board game, but the price seemed a little steep for the product. So as moms on a budget do, I set out to make something that would be just as useful for introducing numbers to my little guy. I ended up with a comparable DIY math peg board game for $12.50.

I want to be able to tap into Samuel's innate need to learn numbers so I'm going to try to present as many activities as I can to help him learn his numbers, counting, and beginning mathematics.

I decided to make my boards 3 inches by 6 inches. This allowed me to use only half of my foam board. (Left over foam board for another project: Bonus!)

I used my cutting boards and rotatory cutter to cut 10 pieces out of 12 inches of my foam board.

I measured 1/2 inch down from the top of each piece and stencilled in each number in the center of each board.

Then I colored in each number with permanent marker.

I measured the center of the boards to align the holes. I made a mark with my pencil to be sure my end product would look the way I wanted it to. Then I used the end of my needle nosed pliers to push through the foam board to make a small hole. I did the same thing on the opposite side. Once I had a hole all the way through, I pushed one of the wooden pegs through the board to be sure the hole was large enough. I cleaned up the back of the holes with some scissors.

Last, I painted the ends of my pegs with different colored paint. I think you could skip this step with no problem.

Presenting this activity is very easy. Have your child roll out his mat and set out the activity. Show how each peg is placed into the holes. Reiterate the fact that one peg is on the board for the number one. Make the same comparison for other boards.

Additionally, you can count the pegs with your child as they place them in the holes. Samuel also liked having the same color pegs for one number. For example, all five red pegs were placed in the number five board or two green pegs in the number two board. This is another sorting activity for your child.

Marie Mack - Child Led Life

Marie is an educator (and former Black Hawk pilot) turned work-at-home mom who blogs about her family's adventures in a child led life at ChildLedLife.com. She shares fun activities for kids, parenting tips, help with homeschool setup, great product reviews, and more. http://childledlife.com/

Jelly Bean Candy Science Experiment

Color Learning, Science, Science Experiments

Toddler

Pre-school

Kinder-garten

You will need:

Jelly beans
Plastic beakers... but you can also use clear cups or bowls
Tap water
Spoons
Plastic tray

How to:

We love simple candy science experiments at my house. I have kids from 2yr - 6yr. Candy science is fun for multiple ages. The little ones just like being involved and the older ones have more hypotheses and ideas for testing. Candy science is a great way to expose the little ones to the ideas of science early on. Simple cause and effect can be seen by even the young. The older ones are gathering more information and developing their own critical thinking from these simple experiments. I love to hear what they think will happen to the candy when we start a candy experiment. It will melt, it will grow, it will disappear, it will change...

Simple science is a fun way to enjoy our afternoons at home. They are usually easy to set up and a no fuss clean up. We often find ways to turn our candy science into sensory play when the experiment is over. This extends our experiment into playtime giving us a fun way to use up our afternoons. Simple science also comes in handy on those rainy, cold, or extremely hot days when you cannot get outside.

First, we set our plastic beakers on the plastic tray. Next, we got out our pack of jelly beans and color sorted them. We wanted to have the jelly jeans tested by color. We had 4 colors to test: purple, blue, white, and light blue. Now we added tap water to our beakers. We did not have a magic volume of water. We just poured the water in until it came up enough to cover the jelly beans. Once the water was in the beakers the kids added the 3 separate colors of jelly beans to its own beaker. This way only one color jelly bean was in each beaker.

Now the watching and waiting part comes in. We sat there watching and talking about what might happen to our candy jelly beans. While talking the kids noticed the water turning the same color as the jelly beans they put in. Note that the white jelly beans did not change the color of the water. We left the jelly beans in the water about an hour and came back to further investigate. The kids noticed the jelly beans had changed the color of the water (all except the white jelly beans) and given the water a scent. They also noticed the coating of the jelly beans had come off while under the water. They went on to mix the water and jelly beans up with a spoon. These jelly beans never dissolved completely. The outer coating did. Finally we scooped out the jelly beans and left the color and scented water in the beakers. We took this water and created paints for more afternoon fun.

FROGS SNAILS AND PUPPY DOG TAILS

Jaime Williams - Frogs and Snails and Puppy Dog Tail

Hi! I am Jaime, mama to three high energy boys. With three boys, life never slows down, but I wouldn't have it any other way! We love creating, learning, and crafting together and we can turn anything into an adventure.
http://frogsandsnailsandpuppydogtail.com/

Easy Volcano Experiment

Science, Science Experiments

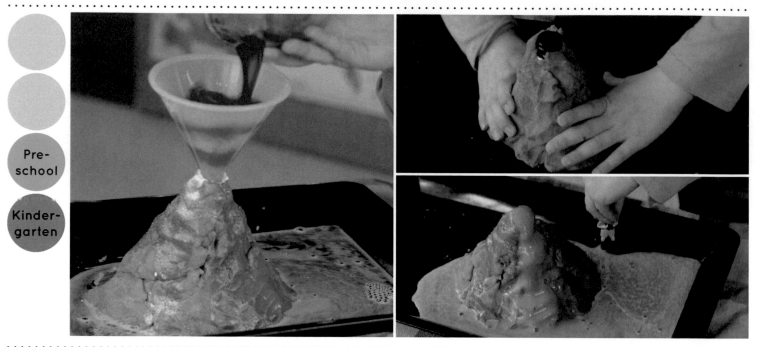

Pre-school

Kinder-garten

You will need:

For the Volcano
Easy no-cook play dough:
2 cup flour
1 cup salt
2 tablespoon oil
2 tablespoon cream of tartar
1.5 cups boiling water
Washable paint or food coloring

For each lava explosion, you will need:
1/2 cup vinegar
2 tablespoon liquid dish soap
red food coloring
1/2 cup baking soda
an empty plastic or glass bottle (we used a cough medicine bottle)
a funnel and a tray

How to:

We love easy, simple science experiments that we can do right in our kitchen. This volcano experiment required two easy recipes that even very young kids can help put together. Once you have the volcano set up, you can create lava explosions over and over again.

First, we mixed up our play dough by putting everything into our stand mixer (except the paint/food coloring). Once the dough was mixed well, we added washable tempera paint in brown. We chose paints since brown is a hard color to get with food coloring. Because the paint is washable, it didn't stain the mixer blade.

You can skip the step of making the dough if you have other play dough on hand. This project would be great for upcycling that lump of play dough we all have where the kids mixed up the colors and it's a brownish gray mass.

Once, the dough was ready, my son began forming it around the empty medicine bottle into the shape of a mountain. Now it was ready for some volcanic action!

In one bowl, we put plain baking soda. In a second bowl, we combined the vinegar, dish soap and food coloring.

Placing the funnel into the top of the "mountain"/bottle, my son first dumped the baking soda in, then the vinegar mixture. Instant lava!

Since the explosion carries out all the ingredients, it leaves the bottle empty so you can keep creating explosions over and over again. My son added some toy people and animals and set up a pretend play scene about escaping lava.

The Science Behind It:
The baking soda reacts with the vinegar to produce a gas: carbon dioxide. The gas builds up enough pressure to force the liquid out of the top of the bottle. The bubbles from the soap help carry the mixture down over the sides of the volcano.

Julie Kirkwood - Creekside Learning

Julie is a homeschooling mom to three, the wife of an amazing cook, a dog rescuer, an explorer of suburban creeks, a sipper of perpetually cold coffee. She and her family live near Washington, D.C.
http://creeksidelearning.com/

Creekside Learning

Learn Your Name Parking Garage

Literacy, Reading

You will need:

Roll of wrapping paper (plain or car themed)
Index cards (one for each letter in your child's name)
Marker

How to:

Are you looking for a way to have your child practice spelling their name? Do you have an abundance of toy cars and trucks in your house? Then this is the activity for you!

It seems like every time I walked into my son's room, I end up stepping on a toy car or truck. If I asked him to clean them up, they ended up in a heap in the middle of the room! So, we came up with a plan to organize the vehicles and sneak in a little learning too.

To help my son organize his collection of cars and trucks, I came up with this parking garage idea. I created three garages out of wrapping paper cut into rectangular pieces. The size of your rectangles will vary based on the length of your child's name.

Then, I used index cards to write each letter of his first, middle and last name. You can write the first letter of each name in a different color to emphasize that it is a capital letter.

On each garage I taped the letters to form parking spots in the garage. I then laminated the garage at a local parent/teacher supply store for durability.

Next step was to attach the garages to the wall. I found that using masking tape or painter's tape worked the best for this step. I have even used Command Strips which work well.

My son was ready to park his cars! As he drove each car to its parking spot, he would say the letter in that spot. To kick the learning up a notch, you could also have your child say the sound that the letter represents. This activity could be adapted for older children by having each card in the garage be a sight word, spelling list word, or vocabulary word. As they park each car, they could say and/or spell the word in that spot.

This has been a great way for my son to practice letter recognition and to learn how to spell his name. Best of all, if I say clean up your cars and trucks, I now walk into a nice organized room!

Jodie Rodriguez - Growing Book by Book

Jodie Rodriguez has a passion for helping caregivers nurture our youngest readers. As a former National Board Certified early-childhood teacher and administrator she has worked with thousands of families and educators providing best literacy practices. She now stays home with home with her two young sons (ages 2 and 4) and is the creator/founder of Growing Book by Book. http://growingbookbybook.com/

The People on The Bus

Math, Counting

Toddler

Pre-school

Kinder-garten

Printable

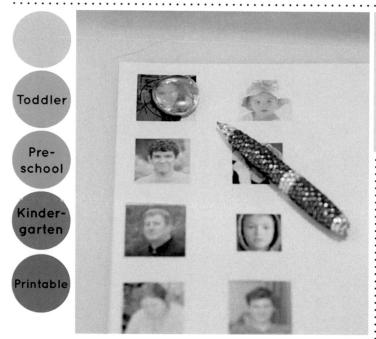

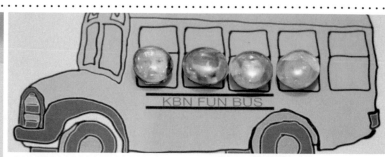

Level 1: Put varying numbers of "people" into the windows of the bus, counting the bus riders each time. For example, you might say, "We're going to put Cassie, Helen and Jared on the bus. Let's find out how many people are riding the bus!" Then count them with your child.

Level 2: Next you might say, "Now Helen has to get off the bus. Let's find out how many people are still on the bus!"

As the child masters basic counting, you can move on to more difficult word problems:

"Cassie, Helen, Jared, and Leo are on the bus, so four people are on the bus. Let's count them. One, two, three, four. How many people are on the bus? Yes, four people."
"Now the bus is at Leo's house. Let's take Leo off the bus. How many people are still on the bus? Yes! There are still three people on the bus!"
"Now Cassie gets off the bus. How many people are still on the bus? How many people got off the bus?"

Start with very small numbers (less than five) and work up as your child masters the skills.

Level 3: As your child gets increasingly skilled with adding and subtracting the bus riders that he or she can see, try covering the bus with construction paper after counting the children.

For example, you might tell your child, "Cassie, Helen, Jared, Leo, Rex and Felix are on the bus." Show the child the bus and count them together, or have the child tell you how many children are on the bus. Now cover the bus with the piece of construction paper. Remove a passenger or two and then ask, "Now how many people are on the bus?"

This helps your child move gently from the concrete to the abstract as he or she imagines the people rather than being able to touch and feel them.

This is also a good time to start asking, "How many seats are left on the bus?" or "How many MORE people can fit on the bus?" making sure that your child knows that there are ten seats altogether. This helps familiarize your child with the "compliments" of ten, that is matching seven empty seats with three filled seats, five empty seats with five filled seats, or four empty seats with six filled seats.

You will need:

Clear flat marbles (available at Michaels or any craft store)
Clear drying glue (I've used Aileene's and clear silicone. Elmer's might also work)
Flat magnets, Cookie sheet
Thumbnail-sized pictures of 10 children (your own children or cut from a magazine, etc.)

One piece of construction paper, heavy paper, cardboard, or another cookie sheet (anything that can hide half or all of the bus riders when your child reaches a level that he or she can do some or all of the math in his or her head).

How to:

Lay a flat marble on top of one of the pictures. Trace around the flat marble. Cut out the round shape and glue the picture to the flat side of the marble, face up. Glue a magnet to the back of the picture, as shown. Repeat for the other nine pictures. Print out school bus and lay on a cookie sheet.

Whew! If you gave up on the flat marble people, don't feel bad! You could just as easily draw a happy face onto a round magnet or use small Lego guys. Believe me, I've done it that way and kids STILL love it! You may have noticed that I included our two cats for mine.

This activity will involve solving word problems at the most basic level and working with your child to add and subtract numbers up to ten in his or her head.

Jill Morgenstern - Do Try This at Home

Jill Morgenstern has a Master's Degree in teaching reading and 13 years of teaching experience. She writes about her family and the ridiculous at http://DoTryThisAtHome.net

Button Bingo

Color Learning, Shapes

Toddler

Pre-school

You will need:

Assortment of buttons
Copy machine
Bingo manipulatives

How to:

Everyone loves a good game of Bingo! Button Bingo is a fun DIY activity that sneaks in some learning concepts; it is a great way to reinforce shapes and colors!

I grabbed 12 buttons of various shapes and colors and used 9 for each Bingo sheet. I made four different game boards and rotated the pieces around for each one.

To make the game board, I placed 9 buttons on our copier (part of our printer.) Place a sheet of white paper on top of the buttons, then close your copier/printer and push your "copy" button.

I put the 12 buttons that were used in a paper bag and had the kiddos take turns pulling out a button. If you have the button on your game board, place a manipulative on that shape. Continue playing until someone calls, "Bingo!"

Kristina Couturier - School Time Snippets

Kristina is a home-schooling mother to four and the creator of the blog, School Time Snippets, where she shares learning and play activities for her children ranging in ages from baby stage to early elementary.
http://www.schooltimesnippets.com/

Painter's Tape Number Hop

Sensory, Gross Motor, Math, Counting

Toddler

Pre-school

Kinder-garten

You will need:

A space on the floor
Painter's tape (easy to remove)
Ball (optional)

How to:

Getting kids excited about math can sometimes be a challenge. Children learn best when their bodies are engaged as well as their minds. With this simple game, they'll be having so much fun they won't even notice they're learning!

Start by clearing a space on the floor. Form numbers on the floor with the Painter's Tape. Space them close enough together that the child can hop between them. Place them out of order if the child is working on number recognition.

There are various ways to play with the numbered floor. Call out a number and have the child hop to it, or the child can take the lead and announce what numbers they hop to. See if the child can hop from 1 all the way up to 10. They could get down on all fours and twist around so that their hands and feet are on the different numbers called out to them. Using a ball, the child can toss the ball at the assigned number.

This simple game is highly adaptable for different learning levels. Challenge the child to follow a sequence or pattern of numbers. When children move beyond the stage of learning number recognition, have them "hop out" different equations. Example: Jump from the 2 to the 3 and then on the 5 while saying "2 plus 3 equals 5."

Julie Nixon - My Mundane and Miraculous Life

Julie is a frazzled mom of two tornadoes, at least one of which has special needs. As a dorky second-generation homeschooler, she writes about learning and play, natural living and matters of the heart. She serves an astounding God that radically saved her. http://www.mymundaneandmiraculouslife.com/

Calendar Time

Color Learning, Shapes, Literacy, Reading, Writing, ABC

Toddler

Pre-school

You will need:

Poster board
Clear page protectors
Construction paper
Stick on velcro pieces
Glue or tape

How to:

As a former elementary school teacher, I know the power of daily reinforcement of skills.

As a mama of two toddlers, I know how difficult that can be. When the elementary school teacher and the mama in me collided, this is what came out.

My little one (2.5 years old) has been learning her letters, numbers, shapes, colors, days of the week and more. I wanted to come up with an idea that would allow me to continue reinforcing and reviewing what we have learned in a way that was fun and engaging.

First, you want to think of the skills that you intend to reinforce with your little one. We are doing shapes, letters, numbers, colors, Spanish words and sign language. That meant that we needed to have five pockets (I combined the shapes and colors). I used clear page protectors and cut them up into pieces that fit my board. Then, I taped them together to make see through pockets. Once you have created the pockets, tape or glue them on to your board.

Next, create your calendar section. In your calendar section, write the days of the week, leaving a box for each day. In those boxes, put one or two Velcro pieces. This will be where you add different activities.

Once the calendar is finished, create the 'flash cards' that go inside each pocket. You will also create a few little squares to put on the different days of the week. Think of activities that you commonly do, such as; the library, Bible study, visit grandparents.
Once you have put it all together and have your calendar ready, put it in a high traffic place in your house. Ours is right beside our dining table, so when we are eating or just finished eating, we can go over it.

I have more ideas on my blog of how to add movement and other activities to keep this interesting as your little one gets older.

Make sure to keep your little one stimulated by constantly adding new material, as well as reviewing the older stuff.

Becky Moseley - Tales of Beauty for Ashes

Becky traded in her teaching degree for diapers and dishes. Her blog, Tales of Beauty for Ashes, has tricks for anything from how to potty train a toddler, be a happier wife or even better ways to organize measuring cups.
http://talesofbeautyforashes.com/

Stack the Erasers Game

Fine Motor, Math, Counting

Pre-school

You will need:

Mini-erasers
Die

How to:

Stack the Erasers game is simple to set-up, works on fine motor skills and counting, and can be a great way to involve siblings of varying ages.

To play, you'll need to gather a set of mini-erasers and a six-sided die. The goal is to see how high you can stack the erasers before it falls over.

Simply start by having one player roll the die and stack that many erasers in the center of the table. Continue rolling the die and adding mini-erasers to the tower. Once it comes tumbling down, start a new game!

Kristina Couturier - School Time Snippets

Kristina is a home-schooling mother to four and the creator of the blog, School Time Snippets where she shares learning and play activities for her children ranging in ages from baby stage to early elementary.
http://www.schooltimesnippets.com/

Color Block Sorting Activity

Milestone Encouragement, Fine Motor, Busy Bags, Color Learning, Math, Counting

Toddler

Pre-school

You will need:

Containers or wooden crates
Colored blocks in four different colors
Colored paper to match the colors of the blocks

How to:

Busy bag activities are a great way to encourage many skills. Busy bags are a reusable and simple way for kids to play over and over again while learning and working on fine motor skills. Typically, busy bag activities are stored in a bag or container and can be pulled out when a child needs a quiet time task while waiting at a restaurant.

This color sorting busy bag activity allows children to sort colored blocks while working on color and shape identification, eye-hand coordination, fine motor skills, visual memory, and visual scanning.

Start by cutting the paper to fit your containers. We used wooden crates for our sorting activity, so rectangles fit the bottom of the crates worked. If you are using bowls, cut the paper into circles. You'll want the base of the containers to hold the paper.

Scatter the colored blocks around and begin the sorting activity by showing the child how to sort the colored blocks into the containers.

Looking around at the scattered blocks allows a child to work on their visual scanning. The child needs to scan and examine the surface with many colored blocks, while focusing and fixating their eyes on the specific colors. This pattern of fixations and saccades of the eyes is a necessary organized skill required for tasks such as reading and writing. Visual perceptual skills are closely related to eye-hand coordination (Eye-hand coordination is defined as using the hands in a coordinated manner in conjunction with the movements of the eyes. Visual input guides reaching and grasping of the hands in functional activities).

Encourage language in this activity by asking questions such as "What shape is this block?"
"What color goes into this crate?"

This activity can be adjusted for older children by asking the child to count the number of blocks in each container or by providing simple addition problems ("How many blocks are in the yellow bin and the green bin all together?")

Colleen Beck, OTR/L - Mommy Needs a Coffee Break

Colleen Beck, OTR/L is the author and creator of a blog where busy moms can find quick and easy busy bag activities, inspiration, and a connection with real moms who need a mini-me time coffee break. She is a busy mom of four and has been an occupational therapist for 15+ years. http://www.mommyneedsacoffeebreak.com/

Chalkboard Letters

Fine Motor, Literacy, Reading, Writing, ABC

Toddler

Pre-school

Kinder-garten

You will need:

Wooden letter set
Chalkboard paint

How to:

These easy to make letters are sure to become a favorite teaching tool. They can be used in a variety of ways with individual children or groups of children at different skill levels. Best of all, the children will be learning in the best possible way - through PLAY!

There are a couple of ways you can create your own set of letters. I made my first set using a brush on chalkboard paint but if you'd like a faster alternative I'd recommend chalkboard spray paint. Place your letters on a piece of wax paper (for easy removal after the paint dries) and give them a coat of paint (as recommended on the label). If you place your letters fairly close to each other you will minimize the amount of paint overspray. You will probably need a couple of coats for good coverage and durability. I suggest that you paint both sides of reversible letters like A, D, E, H, etc. but with letters like C, F, G, J, you use a contrasting paint on the backside. This makes the letters self-correcting so that children can instantly recognize when the letter is backwards. I'd also recommend you do your spray painting outdoors as it can get messy.

When your paint is good and dry, you're all ready to play! Here's some activity ideas to get you started.

Printing Letters
Provide the letters and some chalk. Children trace the letter shapes right onto the letters. It takes practice to get the chalk to stay on the letter. Some children like to color in the whole letter and that's okay, too. As they print or color in the letter, I like to comment on the letters. "That's an 'A' - it has two straight lines joined at the top and another across the middle. 'A' says /a/." I start with short vowel sounds but you could adapt it to suit your own style.

Alphabet Hunt
Hide the letters around the room and have the children find them. If they don't know the names of the letters, then provide the names as they discover and bring them to you. If they can recognize the letters, you could give them specific letters to hunt and ask them not to bring out the letters until you have asked for them by name. With this advanced version, they will be learning self-regulation and memory skills as well, since they have to hold themselves back from bringing the wrong letters and will want to remember where they have seen the letters that haven't been called yet. You could also ask them to find the letter by the sound it makes.

What's Missing?
Place a selection of letters on the table and ask the children to study them. You should choose letters that the children are familiar with and vary the number with their ability. So you might start with only 5 letters and as the children get better with the game you might have 12 or more. Have the children hide their eyes while you remove a few letters. Then ask the children, which letters are missing. Replace the letters as they are named, then play another round.

Run Along A, B, C's
This is a fun way to get the kids moving as they learn. Place the A, B, C's in order along the floor indoors or outdoors on a nice day. Have the children follow along the letters until they get to the end. You could vary the movement. Run to A, hop to B, swim to C, etc. You might choose to have a surprise waiting at the end of the path for a bit of added fun.

Trace the Letter
Instead of printing on the letter, use the letters as templates and trace around them. You could do this outside on the sidewalk or inside on paper. You could also use crayons, markers or pencils instead of chalk.

Suzanne Schlechte - My Buddies and I

Suzanne has over 20 years as a Family Child Care Provider and happily shares those experiences on her blog, "My Buddies and I". There's always something to be learned and Suzanne is on a quest for knowledge and new skills and she hopes to inspire others along the way. http://mybuddiesandi.blogspot.ca/

Alphabet Soup

Literacy, Reading, ABC

Toddler

Pre-school

Kinder-garten

You will need:

Chalkboard letters (can use any other alphabet letters)
Cooking pot
Spoon

How to:

This is a fun game to play with a group of children. It's especially good for children of different ages and skill levels. Place your chalkboard letters around your cooking pot and tell the children you're going to be making alphabet soup together. The children can take turns stirring the pot and selecting what letter to add to the soup pot. A song I like to sing loosely follows the tune of "London Bridge" and it goes like this:

Alphabet Soup Song
We are making alphabet soup, alphabet soup, alphabet soup.
We are making alphabet soup,

(Child's Name) put in an (name the letter the child chooses to add).

Keep singing and adding letters for as long as the children are interested. In a mixed skill level group, the children will learn from each other as the letters are named. If your child, or group of children are more advanced, you can increase the skill level by naming specific letters for the them to find to put in the pot and switch the last line in the song to "Who can find the (name letter)."

This activity is great to add to a cooking theme, and can work well as a review or informal assessment to get an idea of what the children know. You can add to the activity by serving bowls of alphabet cereal or alphabet crackers for snack.

Suzanne Schlechte - My Buddies and I

Suzanne has over 20 years as a Family Child Care Provider and happily shares those experiences on her blog, "My Buddies and I". There's always something to be learned and Suzanne is on a quest for knowledge and new skills and she hopes to inspire others along the way. http://mybuddiesandi.blogspot.ca/

Spelling Practice Templates

Literacy, Reading, ABC

Toddler

Pre-school

Kinder-garten

You will need:

Chalkboard letters (can use any other alphabet letters)
Paper or cardstock
Marker or pencil
Chalk

How to:

Choose some simple words and create templates for them on paper or cardstock by tracing around each of the chalkboard letters. You may decide to laminate the cards if you would like them to be really durable.

Children can select a card and add the corresponding chalkboard letter to the template. After creating the word, they can use chalk to print on the chalkboard letter for extra practice.

As children increase in skill you may want to create a second or third set of chalkboard letters so that you may create increasingly complex words. The children may even decide to create their own word templates.

Here's some ideas for words using a single set of chalkboard letters just to get you started:

at	et	in	op	ub	ad	ed	it	ot	un
bat	bet	bin	hop	cub	bad	bed	bit	cot	bun
cat	get	fin	mop	hub	dad	fed	fit	dot	fun
fat	jet	pin	top	rub	had	led	hit	hot	gun
hat	let	tin		sub	lad	red	lit	not	run
mat	met				sad	wed	pit	lot	sun
pat	pet						sit	pot	
sat	set								
rat									
vat									

Suzanne Schlechte - My Buddies and I

Suzanne has over 20 years as a Family Child Care Provider and happily shares those experiences on her blog, "My Buddies and I". There's always something to be learned and Suzanne is on a quest for knowledge and new skills and she hopes to inspire others along the way. http://mybuddiesandi.blogspot.ca/

Reverse Reading Game

Literacy, Reading

Toddler

Pre-school

Kinder-garten

You will need:

Chalkboard alphabet letters (can use any other alphabet letters)

How to:

This is a really great game to help beginner readers who struggle with sounding out words. Lay out your chalkboard letters and tell your child you are going to have them spell words by giving them the sounds and they will find the matching letter. Then take apart a simple word into the letter sounds. So CAT becomes /c/ /a/ /t/. Don't say the word, and be sure to pause between each letter sound. The child should place the letters CAT on the table. You may have to correct them if they use an alternate letter (such as K instead of C) but this is just extra practice.

Now it is up to your child to push the sounds together in their mind to hear the word. You may need to repeat the sounds a few times individually until the child understands how it works. The skill of putting the sounds together doesn't come naturally to all children, and that can cause reading difficulties. If your child struggles with the words, keep repeating the sounds closer together to help them "hear" the word. They will improve as they develop the skill to combine the individual sounds into words.

You can also play this as a travel game without using the chalkboard letters, just sounding out the word letter by letter. I like to pick words from the things we see on our journey as words. As children improve you can use more complicated words with many sounds.

Suzanne Schlechte - My Buddies and I

Suzanne has over 20 years as a Family Child Care Provider and happily shares those experiences on her blog, "My Buddies and I". There's always something to be learned and Suzanne is on a quest for knowledge and new skills and she hopes to inspire others along the way. http://mybuddiesandi.blogspot.ca/

Alphabet Treasure Hunt

Sensory, Literacy, ABC

Pre-school

You will need:

Flour
Vegetable oil
Glass stones
Permanent marker
Empty wipes container - optional

How to:

My son loves to go on treasure hunts so I developed this fun, sensory alphabet hunt to help him practice letter recognition and letter sounds. He really loved the activity and I was very pleased with how much learning took place too.

The first thing you need to do is write one letter on each glass stone with permanent marker. These can be used again and again for other activities as well. Then make a list of the letters they will be searching for on a sheet of paper.

After that, you will make the sand. It is actually cloud dough with a slight beige tint that resembles sand. It adds an additional sensory experience to the activity and raised the fun level for my son. In order to make the cloud dough, you will mix 8 cups of flour with 1 cup of vegetable oil. Stir it together until all of the flour is mixed with the oil. Then pour it into a plastic bin.

Now you can add the letter gems to the cloud dough. Mix it all around so the letters are hidden all throughout the bin. Lay the alphabet list right next to the bin. If you would like to include a treasure box, you will need to place an empty wipes container or some other box next to the bin as well.

Then instruct your child to look through the dough to find the letter gems. When they find a gem they should name the letter out loud and also say the sound the letter makes. After that, they can cross the letter off of the list. Finally, they will add the letter gem to their treasure box. This continues until all of the letters are found and marked off the list.

Danielle Buckley - Mom Inspired Life

Danielle is a wife and a stay-at-home mom to her two young children. They are the inspiration for writing the blog, Mom Inspired Life. As a former educator, she enjoys the process of teaching her own children and watching them learn new things daily. She loves creating learning activities that excite and inspire a love of learning in them. http://mominspiredlife.com/

Circle Tray for Pre-Writing Practice

Milestone Encouragement, Fine Motor, Writing

Toddler

Pre-school

You will need:

Wooden or metal task tray
Medium size pom-poms (4 of each color)
Fine motor tweezers or tongs
Silicon ice cube tray (or small muffin tin)
Small wooden bowl

How to:

Place the medium size pom-poms in the small wooden bowl. Include the wooden bowl, fine motor tweezers, and silicon ice cube tray on the wooden task tray, as pictured.

Encourage your child to use the fine motor tweezers with the fingers they use to hold a pencil: the thumb, pointer and middle finger. The 4th and 5th finger should be tucked inside their palm. This helps them to strengthen the finger muscles needed for a proper pencil grasp later in handwriting.

Then show them how to use the fine motor tweezers to move the pom-poms from the small wooden bowl into the holes in the silicon ice tray. You can also use a small muffin tin if you can't find a silicon ice tray.

They can choose to put all the same colored pom-poms in the same row, or do a pattern. Once you show them how to complete the activity, try to sit back and let them finish it as they wish.

Developmentally, kids start to form a correct circle shape by the time they are three. However, from ages 2 and on, they are able to make circular motions with any type of writing utensil or their fingers.

My daughter began showing increased interest in shapes, especially the circle shape, at around 20-24 months old. She began to make circular motions using a crayon or small pencil at 26 months old. However each child is different, so some may show interest sooner or later.

This activity helps to engage them in an interest of shapes, while introducing them to some basic pre-writing skills they will need later for handwriting.

Some other great skills your child is practicing with this activity are:
Color recognition
Patterns (to include patterns put one pom-pom of each color in the first space and then allow your child to fill in the rest)
Beginning one-to-one correspondence skills
Fine motor strengthening for proper pencil grasp development
Crossing midline (the arm moving across the middle of their body to grab a pom-pom with the fine motor tweezers using their dominate hand).

Heather Greutman - Golden Reflections Blog

Heather Greutman is a homeschool graduate turned homeschool mom blogger. She worked as an Occupational Therapy Assistant in the public school system before becoming a stay-at-home mom to her daughter. She enjoys sharing her tot-school and preschool ideas on her blog, GoldenReflectionsBlog.com where she writes about Christian Montessori inspired homeschool with an Occupational Therapy twist. http://goldenreflectionsblog.com/

Number Sensory Bin

Sensory, Counting

Toddler

Pre-school

You will need:

We used apple scented cloud dough as our sensory bin filler (8 cups of flour and 1 cup of cooking oil will give you cloud dough) that we had leftover from another play activity.
Foam numbers
Bin or large bowl
Plastic tablecloth (optional)

How to:

We love sensory play and learning at my house. Setting up a sensory bin or sensory activity is often something all 3 of my multi-aged children can enjoy. Sensory play is a hands-on way of learning through our senses. Our senses are touch, sight, smell, taste, and sound. Depending on what we are playing with, the taste option might not always be available, but sight and touch are easy to include in so many play activities. There are also many ways to include learning while playing. That is just what we did with our Number Sensory Bin. The kids got to explore with their senses as well as go over number recognition, counting out loud, and matching up number sequences with the foam numbers. A fun afternoon spent playing while learning was a hit for us.

If you do not have left over cloud dough or another sensory bin filler you would like to use, make cloud dough to start. It is very easy. Just mix the flour and oil together until it is moldable. You can add color with powdered paint or chalk or you can added scents with oils. Plain cloud dough is amazing on its own. Now take a clear plastic bin or large bowl and add cloud dough to it.

Next, you take the foam numbers and bury them inside the bin. I placed the number sensory bin on a plastic tablecloth outside to try and contain the mess a little. Now, it was time to play and learn.

Once the bowl or bin was down, my 2yr old and 3yr old were ready to start exploring. My 3yr old dug out all of the numbers and we talked about each one as he went along. He made a stack of numbers on the tablecloth. We then started to count 1-10. After that, I suggested we see if we could put them on the tablecloth in the order they went. We started with 1 and got to 9 and then he had to use the 1 and 0 to make 10. This was a simple learning activity to go along with playtime.

I think hands-on learning while playing is so much fun to try with my kids. Little brother really enjoyed counting while playing. Baby brother had a lot of fun digging his hands through the cloud dough. Our "Number Sensory Bin" was a hit. Since the cloud dough keeps well in a plastic zipped bag, I can see us using this activity over and over until the cloud dough is gone.

We hope you can have fun with this idea too.

FROGS SNAILS AND PUPPY DOG TAILS

Jaime Williams - Frogs and Snails and Puppy Dog Tail

Hi! I am Jaime, mama to three high energy boys. With three boys, life never slows down, but I wouldn't have it any other way! We love creating, learning, and crafting together and we can turn anything into an adventure.
http://frogsandsnailsandpuppydogtail.com/

Dot the Number Game

Math, Counting

Pre-school

You will need:

Dice
Paper
Pen
Dot markers or dot stickers

How to:

This game is so simple to set up, but very effective at teaching counting and number recognition to preschoolers. One round of the game only takes about 5 minutes, so you can play it even when you are limited on time. If you are a teacher, this would be a great game to include in your math centers too.

Write the numbers 1-6 in rows across the paper. I include 5 or 6 rows of numbers. I don't write them all in order, just to keep my son from simply memorizing the location of each number. You could also use this game to practice numbers 7-12, or even higher, by using 2 or more dice.

Each player will get a different color do a dot marker or different color dot stickers.

How To Play Dot the Number

Your child will roll the die (dice). They will count the dots facing up on the die.

Then find that number on the paper and dot it with a do a dot marker or place a dot sticker on it. The next player does goes

through steps 1-3.

This repeats until someone has dotted all the numbers in one row.

Not only does this game help kids learn to count and identify numbers, but it also helps to develop critical thinking skills. They have to think about where to place their dot so that they have the best chance of filling up a row first.

My son and I enjoy playing this game together and I love that he is learning so much while we play it!

Danielle Buckley - Mom Inspired Life

Danielle is a wife and a stay-at-home mom to her two young children. They are the inspiration for writing the blog, Mom Inspired Life. As a former educator, she enjoys the process of teaching her own children and watching them learn new things daily. She loves creating learning activities that excite and inspire a love of learning in them.
http://mominspiredlife.com/

Follow the ABC Trail

Fine Motor, Gross Motor, Literacy, Reading, ABC

Pre-school

Kinder-garten

You will need:

26 poker chips
1 permanent marker
2 baskets

How to:

Little ones have lots of energy! We are always looking for gross motor activities to get some of the wiggles out and at the same time work on building literacy skills.

Follow the ABC Trail is a fun alphabet version of the traditional hide-and-seek game that will remind you a bit of the story of Hansel and Gretel. It's the perfect game for two children. This game will help develop fine motor skills, gross motor skills, letter identification, estimation and learning to take turns.

To prepare the game, you will need to make your alphabet chips. We used poker chips and wrote a letter of the alphabet on each one with a permanent marker. You could also use labeled construction paper pieces, milk jug tops or magnetic letters. Place the chips in a basket.

Both players begin at the same location. Player 1 decides on a place to hide. As the child travels to her hiding spot, she drops alphabet chips behind her to form a trail. The player has to be strategic and estimate how much space they should leave between the chips to reach their destination. You don't want to run out of chips before you get to your hiding spot!

Meanwhile, player 2 closes his eyes and recites the alphabet song or says the alphabet two times. Player 2 then follows the trail to the hiding spot. Along the way, he picks up each alphabet chip, names the letter and places it in another basket.

Variation: Children who can identify the letters of the alphabet may enjoy naming a word for each letter that they find along the trail. For older children, you could write sight words or spelling words on the chips instead of the letters of the alphabet.

Once player 1 is discovered, the players switch roles and play again.

Play continues until someone tires. In our house, the kids can easily play the game for 30 minutes.

Jodie Rodriguez - Growing Book by Book

Jodie Rodriguez has a passion for helping caregivers nurture our youngest readers. As a former National Board Certified early-childhood teacher and administrator, she has worked with thousands of families and educators providing best literacy practices. She now stays home with home with her two young sons (ages 2 and 4) and is the creator/founder of Growing Book by Book. http://growingbookbybook.com/

LEGO Math Number Line

Math, Counting

Pre-school

Kinder-garten

You will need:

Assorted LEGO Bricks
1 LEGO mini-figure
Long sheet of easel paper
Marker or crayon

How to:

If your child is learning to count, learning to add or subtract, and is a LEGO fan, this game is perfect. The LEGO Number Line Game uses what you already have to make math fun.

Take a long sheet of paper and draw your number line and the set of numbers you want your child to work with. This game can be played at any math level. We've used it in several ways.

Young preschoolers learning one-to-one correspondence can place a LEGO above each number from 0 to 10.

Older preschoolers learning to count from 1-10, 1-30, 1-50 as they show readiness, can hop their LEGO mini-figure from block to block.

Kindergarteners can hop their figure from 1-100 and begin adding and subtracting. Call out equations to your child (or to the LEGO mini-figure) and have them move the LEGO figure along the number line. ("What's 3+4, LEGO Man?")

If your child is ready to move on, try working with fact families. "How many ways can LEGO Man get 10?" (start at 5 and jump 5 more, start at 6 and jump 4 more and so on).

Keep this activity in mind for working with elementary-aged kids who are learning the concept of negative numbers. Draw your number line to include negative and positive numbers. Give your child numbers to add and subtract that moves them along both the negative and positive parts of the number line.

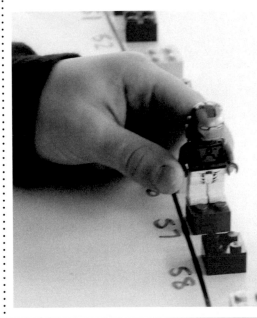

Julie Kirkwood -Creekside Learning

Julie is a homeschooling mom to three, the wife of an amazing cook, a dog rescuer, an explorer of suburban creeks, a sipper of perpetually cold coffee. She and her family live near Washington, DC. http://creeksidelearning.com/

Magic Blossoming Flower

Fine Motor, Science, Science Experiments

Toddler

Pre-school

You will need:

Squares of paper (These can be any size square and any kind of paper. Having an assortment of different weights/thicknesses is ideal so you can observe how they each unfold differently.)
Scissors
Stickers
Bowl of water

How to:

Make flowers out of paper and watch them magically unfold to reveal a surprise! This is a fun activity that preschoolers can do all on their own while working on important fine motor skills like cutting with scissors and folding paper neatly.

Fold the paper in half one way and then in half the other way. You should end up with a square. Draw a petal shape outward from the folded corner. Cut around the shape to make the petals.

Open up the paper flower. Place a sticker in the center. Fold the tip of each petal to the middle point so that the sticker is hidden.

Gently place the flower in the bowl of water. Watch what happens! Repeat with various kinds of paper that have different thicknesses. Does a tissue paper flower unfold more or less quickly than one made of cardstock?

Your child will be delighted to watch his/her flower "magically" unfold in water to reveal a colorful sticker inside. But is it really magic? Of course not—it's science!

Paper is made up of small fibers. When these fibers absorb water, they swell up and the paper expands. This makes the creases flatten out, which in turn makes the flower open. Different types of paper soak up water at different speeds. A tissue paper flower opens almost immediately on contact with water while a cardstock flower may take a minute or so to slowly blossom.

Crystal Chatterton - The Science Kiddo

Crystal is a homeschooling mom of two blondies. After giving up an academic career in chemistry to stay home with her kids she launched The Science Kiddo to focus on doing science experiments with her children. She blogs about science activities for kids, early childhood science education, homeschool, and urban living.
http://www.sciencekiddo.com/

Preschool Science Lab

Science, Science Experiments

Pre-school

Kinder-garten

You will need:

Cups, bowls, jars, glasses, preferably see-through
Spoons, measuring cups
Droppers or pipettes
Dry kitchen ingredients. We used: baking soda, baking powder, salt, sugar, and corn starch
Liquid kitchen ingredients. We used white vinegar, water, and lemon juice. We also included ice
Towels for clean up or to place under the lab if doing this activity indoors.

How to:

A simple at home science lab using common kitchen ingredients is perfect for preschoolers and kindergarteners but even older kids will love to explore the chemistry of mixing up common household powders and liquids.

The idea behind this lab is to let kids have a little free play with mixing up concoctions. Let them say "Whoa!" and encourage their curiosity instead of prescribing a set of instructions they have to follow. Bonus: there's no way to fail.

Instructions:
Place dry items in separate jars and fill measuring cups with liquids.
Name each item for your child.
Ask him or her to choose one liquid to pour into a dry item and observe the reaction.
Repeat as often as desired, letting the child be the guide.

How much you want to intervene with the mixing process is up to you and the age of your child. I did chat a bit with my 5-year-old on the first go around of mixing. I named each item and we poured a little bit of water in each one to see what happened. Then we repeated this with vinegar, and so forth. After than, my son decided how he would mix each substance depending on how it reacted.

Since children love to mix things that provide a satisfying reaction, allow as much free reign as you can. Preschoolers and kindergarteners don't need to know the scientific explanations about why acids and bases react the way they do. They are at the perfect age where their natural curiosity will take over, establishing a firm foundation for scientific learning in later years.

Activity extensions: Older kids can keep a chart of their observations and record exact measurements used.

Erica - What Do We Do All Day?

Erica is a stay-at-home-mom to two rowdy and creative boys. She blogs about easy at home playful learning activities and creates children's book lists at What Do We Do All Day? http://www.whatdowedoallday.com/

Growing Sweet Potato Vines Indoors

Science, Science Experiments

You will need:

Sweet potato
Toothpicks
Jar
Water
Sunny window

How to:

Observing how some vegetables magically regrow from scraps is a fascinating plant science project you can do at home with the kids even if you don't have a yard. Anyone with a sunny window can, as my boys like to say, "turn garbage into plants."

One of the easiest and most satisfying vegetable to regrow is the humble sweet potato. Next time you let one linger too long on your kitchen counter, grab it for a gardening experiment with the kids.

Cut the sweet potato in half. Insert toothpicks into the side of the sweet potato and rest on the top edge of the jar. Fill jar with water until it just reaches the bottom of the sweet potato. Place in a sunny window.

You will want to check the water every day to make sure it reaches the bottom of the sweet potato. Change the water every few days when it gets cloudy.

Soon, delicate white roots will emerge from the sweet potato and fill the jar and purplish-green leafy stems will push out of the "eyes" of the sweet potato. Kids love to watch as the leafy vines grow longer and longer.

Notes: you can also plant the sweet potato in soil, but watching the roots form is half the fun. If you plant it in soil, the plant will last longer, but we prefer to simply compost the sprouted sweet potato when it gets too big for the jar and start a new one.

Activity Extension Ideas:
Sprout several sweet potato pieces at the same time. Young plant scientists can record their observations on a chart. Have them note down which pieces sprouted roots or vines first, when the first leaves unfurled and how often the water had to be refilled and changed. They can even compare the growth of sweet potatoes planted in soil to those planted in water.

Erica - What Do We Do All Day?

Erica is a stay-at-home-mom to two rowdy and creative boys. She blogs about easy at home playful learning activities and creates children's book lists at What Do We Do All Day? http://www.whatdowedoallday.com/

Reggio-Inspired Preschool Math

Fine Motor, Math, Counting, Shapes, Size Sorting

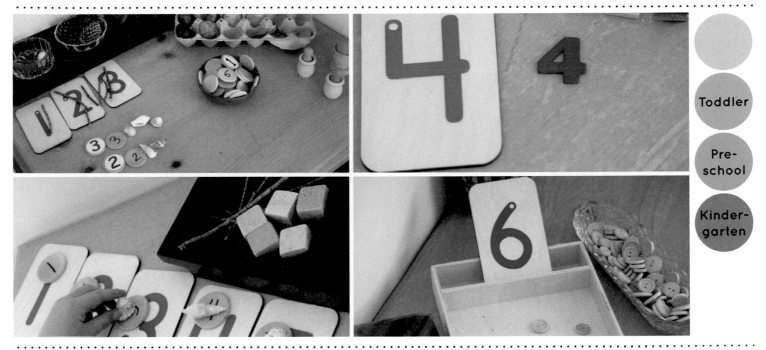

Toddler

Pre-school

Kinder-garten

You will need:

A tray: Any divided tray found at a re-sale shop will be fine. We love searching for beautiful wooden plates or bowls, or a Melissa & Doug divided tray will also work.

Numbers: These may include sandpaper numbers, wooden numerals (we have natural and colored numerals from Michael's), or you can easily create your own by writing numbers on rocks, gems, wooden blocks, or acorns with a permanent marker.

Various small parts: rocks, gems, sticks, craft sticks, pinecones, acorns, mosaic tiles, wooden buttons, blocks, discs or clothespins, seashells.

How to:

The Reggio Emilia approach to early childhood development places value on the innate curiosities of a child. Play time is cognitive learning and should be respected and encouraged. Learning is adapted to the needs and interests of the individual and encourages children to discover answers on their own.

This simple Reggio-inspired math provocation can excite your child about mathematical concepts. A beautiful math tray or work table can inspire children to create and learn about numbers.

An open-ended learning time to explore number sense is simple to set up. To get started, place one number on the tray, and count out that number with various small parts. You can sit with

your child to explain what you've done, or simply leave it there for your child to find and to pique his/her interest. While watching your child, observe what they are doing. It is also fine to work with them to teach them how to count to that number or even create number sentences using the provided tactile objects. I always take notes on what particular objects interest my child most, so I can think of ways to incorporate those again in the future.

Here is a list of mathematic outcomes your child is discovering through this Reggio-inspired math table, and variations thereof: counting and recognizing numbers, learning one-to-one correspondence (number sense), working on patterns and sequencing (ABAB, AABB, AAB), ordering (smallest to largest, etc.) addition, subtraction, comparing objects, classifying and sorting (by size, type, color), spatial relationships, and measurement.

I hope you and your child enjoy a playful and open ended time through this Reggio-inspired number exploration. Our corner table is always set up with either a mathematics provocation, nature exploration, or a literacy table. The possibilities are endless, and since you are using materials from nature or around the house, it doesn't have to cost anything extra! I regularly change out the materials to excite my children's interests. I hope you feel inspired to do the same!

Amy Smith, M.Ed. - Wildflower Ramblings

Amy Smith, M.Ed., is a kindergarten teacher turned stay-at-home mom to her two children. She loves Classical, Montessori, and Reggio-inspired learning and teaching. Amy is a Sergeant First Class in the Army Reserve and blogs at Wildflower Ramblings about homeschooling, sensory play, herbal remedies, and their grace filled lives. http://wildflowerramblings.com/

Alphabet Soup

Literacy, ABC

You will need:

Pot
Soup ladle or spoon
Bowl
Alphabet pieces

How to:

It's a tough job to learn your letters when you're young! But it's an important job as they are everywhere. There are hundreds of ways you can help your child to learn their letters, and this is my personal favorite!

You can use foam puzzle pieces, magnetic letters, or even handwritten letters on pieces of paper, use whatever you have. Choose 3 or 4 letters to start with to make it easy. Put the letters in a pot. You can use toy pots, a real soup pot from the kitchen, or any other item. In the past I have used bowls, or even a brown paper bag will work, just shake it up instead!

Stir up the letters with a spoon singing/chanting:
Alphabet soup, alphabet soup
Stir it up, mix it up
Alphabet soup.

Then ask your child to scoop out a random letter from the pot and identify it. If they are too young, you can say the letter and have them repeat it after you. If they are a little more confident in their letter recognition, they can holler out the letter. The louder they scream the letter, the more fun they have and the

better they remember the letters (this is only my own opinion, but you can try the theory out for yourself).

Toddlers will love to serve up letters for 'lunch'. 'M' for Mommy, 'T' for Tristan, 'D' for Daddy, etc. Make the letters more meaningful by using ones that are in familiar names. These are always the easiest ones for small children to remember.

If you are teaching phonics, you can also make the sound of the letter. Repeat the chant for each letter that is served from the pot.

As your little one's recognition of the letters improves, you can add more letters to the pot to increase the difficulty of the game.

Try having older children pick out the letters to spell their name, or other words. Have fun with this game!

Crystal McClean - Castle View Academy

Crystal is an ex-pat home educating Mama who is passionate about her children, learning, crafting and frugality.
http://www.castleviewacademy.com/

My First Journal - Smash Book Style

Fine Motor, Writing

Toddler

Pre-school

Kinder-garten

You will need:

Journal (i.e. notebook, sketch pad, etc.)
Pencils, markers and/or crayons
Glue stick or tape
Small flat memories (i.e. Movie stubs, postcards, pictures, draw-ings, first scribbles)

How to:

Journaling is so important for kids. It teaches them how to sort through feelings, understand emotions, and problem solve. Replaying what happened yesterday or today also helps them learn more about themselves.

It doesn't have to be complicated. There are almost no rules when it comes to journaling - allow your child to have creative control over their journal. They may express a lot one day and nearly nothing the next. That's ok! The instructions that follow are just to give you some ideas on where to start.

For pre-writing little ones, I like to write for them. That way that can look back and remember the types of thoughts they had in their head. Be careful not to overpower their thoughts by over-suggesting. A great question to begin with is "What's your story about today?" or "Can you tell me the beginning of your story?" Some days they might make-believe; other days they might start a story and never finish it. At this age, that's completely ok! It's just about them expressing their thoughts. I do try to do a structured interview post twice a year, asking them the same set of questions each time.

Another great way to start is by having them draw pictures. Ask them what their picture is and as they describe it to you, write their words in quotes. For example: "He's a scary dinosaur and this is his sharp teeth." I love to write it word for word and include any grammar mistakes they make, rather than correcting them. That way, we can look back later and remember how little they once were!

You can also make some pages Smash Book pages. A Smash Book is basically a messy scrapbook, a really easy way to "smash" memories into a page and not worry about it looking perfect. Some of our favorite memories to tape into our books are postcards, movie stubs, little notes I've written them, birthday cards, and of course pictures!

Kids love the smash-book pages because they are completely in charge of how their memories are put in the book -- there's absolutely no wrong way. Upside down is even ok!

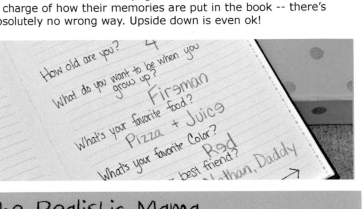

Alida Quittschreiber - The Realistic Mama

The Realistic Mama

Alida is a writer, wife and mama of 1. She runs, The Realistic Mama, a successful blog full of realistic parenting tips, easy recipes, kids activities and more. Her goal is to help moms spend more quality time with their kids in realistic, stress-free ways. She loves chocolate, travel, and getting messy with kids. http://www.therealisticmama.com/

Shape Scavenger Hunt Photo Book

Shapes

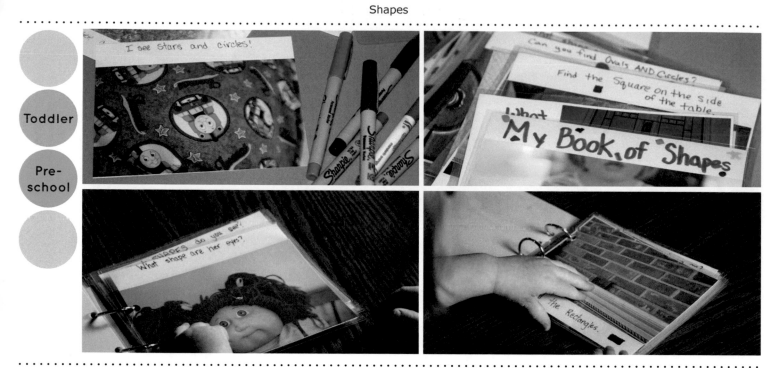

Toddler

Pre-school

You will need:

Digital camera or smart phone
Printer (or you can use a photo printing service)
Cardstock
Markers or pens
Laminator (if desired)
Hole punch
Binding ring(s)

How to:

To make learning shapes into a hands-on project to revisit time and again, take a toddler or preschooler on a shape photo scavenger hunt and create a shape photo book.

The first step is the most fun for the child. Talk about the shape (or shapes) that he or she has learned. Arm the child with a worksheet (such as the sample provided) identifying the shape(s) to look for. Then, begin the hunt with a camera or smart phone. When the child sees a shape in nature, on furniture, or elsewhere in a home or classroom, he or she should take a picture. Explore many rooms, playgrounds, or yards and find interesting patterns on fabrics and toys.

For the youngest children, of course, parents may need to assist in holding the camera and/or focusing on the items. For the most part, however, kids love learning to use a camera, and taking an in-focus picture with a modern-day digital camera is easier to learn than it has ever been. Help the child find the shapes, but let the child be the photographer as much as possible.

Encourage your little photographer to take as many pictures as possible, because the chances are that many will not turn out clear.

After the scavenger hunt, review the images on a computer with your child. My daughter was so excited to see her images on the computer screen!

Next comes the book assembly!

Step 1. Select the clearest pictures to represent each shape and print them (or have them printed).

Step 2. Paste each selected picture to a half-page or square of cardstock, and write directions or reminders on each page. Although my preschool toddler cannot read the text yet, as I "read" with her, it helps her see how her images have illustrated a book, and it is personalized to her. For example, during our scavenger hunt, she had noticed her doll's circle eyes, so that is what I reminded her of on her doll's page.

Step 3. Laminate each page (if desired) for durability.

Step 4. Punch holes on the sides of the pages, slide a binding ring through the holes, and read your book with your child!

My daughter loved her scavenger hunt and enjoys reviewing her shapes by reading her book. It is a good thing that, with the ring binding, it will be easy to add more of her creations. She keeps begging to do another shape scavenger hunt with my camera again!

Rebecca Reid - Line upon Line Learning

Rebecca Reid is a homeschooling stay-at-home mom to two kids, "Raisin" (age 7) and "Strawberry" (age 3). She blogs on parenting, homeschooling, and life-long education at {www.lineuponlinelearning.com} Line upon Line Learning, where she also shares supplementary educational materials for parents and teachers.
http://www.lineuponlinelearning.com/

Make a Felt Story Board

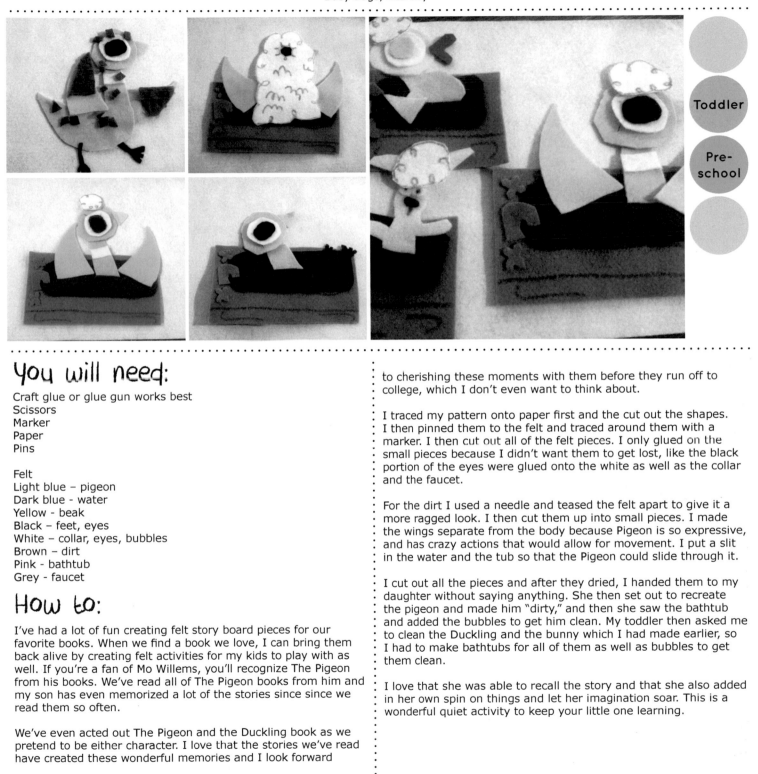

Toddler

Pre-school

You will need:

Craft glue or glue gun works best
Scissors
Marker
Paper
Pins

Felt
Light blue – pigeon
Dark blue - water
Yellow - beak
Black – feet, eyes
White – collar, eyes, bubbles
Brown – dirt
Pink - bathtub
Grey - faucet

How to:

I've had a lot of fun creating felt story board pieces for our favorite books. When we find a book we love, I can bring them back alive by creating felt activities for my kids to play with as well. If you're a fan of Mo Willems, you'll recognize The Pigeon from his books. We've read all of The Pigeon books from him and my son has even memorized a lot of the stories since since we read them so often.

We've even acted out The Pigeon and the Duckling book as we pretend to be either character. I love that the stories we've read have created these wonderful memories and I look forward to cherishing these moments with them before they run off to college, which I don't even want to think about.

I traced my pattern onto paper first and the cut out the shapes. I then pinned them to the felt and traced around them with a marker. I then cut out all of the felt pieces. I only glued on the small pieces because I didn't want them to get lost, like the black portion of the eyes were glued onto the white as well as the collar and the faucet.

For the dirt I used a needle and teased the felt apart to give it a more ragged look. I then cut them up into small pieces. I made the wings separate from the body because Pigeon is so expressive, and has crazy actions that would allow for movement. I put a slit in the water and the tub so that the Pigeon could slide through it.

I cut out all the pieces and after they dried, I handed them to my daughter without saying anything. She then set out to recreate the pigeon and made him "dirty," and then she saw the bathtub and added the bubbles to get him clean. My toddler then asked me to clean the Duckling and the bunny which I had made earlier, so I had to make bathtubs for all of them as well as bubbles to get them clean.

I love that she was able to recall the story and that she also added in her own spin on things and let her imagination soar. This is a wonderful quiet activity to keep your little one learning.

Monique Boutsiv - Living Life and Learning

You can find Monique writing about homeschooling tips, activities and parenting at Living Life and Learning. She is a biology graduate, web designer and homeschools her 3 children. They love notebooking and a relaxed approach to homeschooling. When she's not homeschooling, you'll find her playing around with code and photoshop because she also designs websites. http://www.livinglifeandlearning.com/

Fun Math Game

Color Learning, Math, Counting, Shapes

Toddler

Pre-school

Kinder-garten

You will need:

55 small objects
A bowl to hold small objects
Cards, numbered 1-10, one number per card

How to:

Sorting helps children notice differences in objects and creates an awareness for math. Counting and number recognition are key parts of early math. The child learns these three vital premath activities of sorting, counting and number recognition in one simple game. Moreover, the game is very easy to set up.

To play this fun game, for numbers 1 to 10, take as many same objects the number represents. For example, for number 1 take 1 bead, for number 2 take 2 coins, for number 3 take 3 cheerios etc till number 10. So we need 55 small objects. Write numbers 1 to 10 on small cards. Invite the child to play.

Give the number cards to the child and ask the child to arrange the cards so that the cards can be picked up later pretty easily.

Ask the child to choose one item from the bowl. Talk about how it looks, what color it is, how it feels. Ask the child to keep the item on the mat. Encourage the child to pick the same item from the bowl and keep it on the mat near the previously placed item. Repeat these steps for all the items in the bowl. The child has sorted the items into small groups. By picking the small items from the bowl and placing them on the mat, the child is working on the fine motor skills too.

Start with one of the sorted groups. Ask the child to count the items in the group. Once counted, tell the child to pick the corresponding number from the number cards. Place the card under the items. Now the child is working on counting and number recognition skills. Count the items in all the groups and place them over the corresponding numbers.

Children like small colorful objects. As this game involves colorful small objects, the child will surely love this simple and fun game.

Disclaimer: Though my preschooler does not keep any small object in her mouth, I supervised her carefully throughout the whole activity.

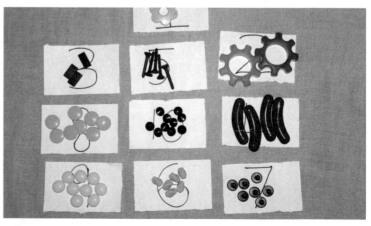

Dhiyana - Edutainment At Home

Dhiyana is a full time Software Engineer, mom to two daughters, wife of an amazing man. She documented the activities she did with her elder daughter in the blog www.dheekshu.blogspot.com. Since it is in her mother tongue, most of her friends could not enjoy those posts. Hence the English blog www.sparklingbuds.blogspot.com was born. She shares art, craft and playful learning ideas in her blog.

Montessori-Inspired Color Graphing

Fine Motor, Color Learning, Math, Counting

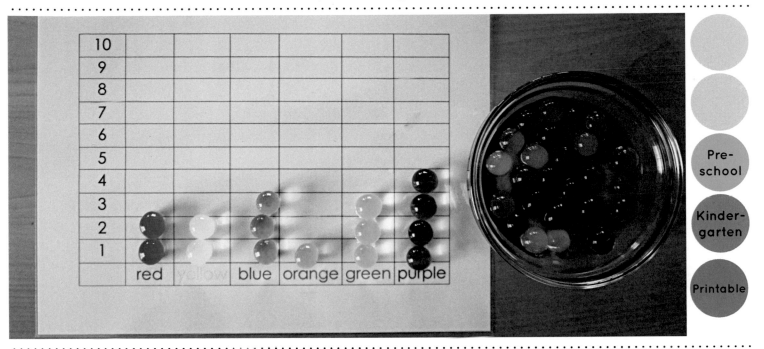

Pre-school

Kinder-garten

Printable

You will need:

Water beads in red, yellow, blue, orange, green, and purple
Bowl with water for hydrated water beads
Color graphing printable
Laminator for printable
Tray to fit printable and bowl of water beads

How to:

I love using water beads for learning activities! There are lots and lots of ways you can use water beads to prepare educational activities, but one of my favorite ways is to prepare a Montessori-inspired graphing activity. Graphing with water beads makes math graphing much more interesting.

You can use this activity to graph color words for multiple ages. Young preschoolers can use the printable and activity to match colors and practice counting. Older preschoolers and kindergarteners can use it to become familiar with a bar graph and learn color words. You can discuss the concept of primary and secondary colors with children who are ready. This is also a hands-on introduction to probability.

Water beads seem to have a life of their own, so this activity is great for working on fine-motor skills as well. It's very difficult to line up the water beads, requiring careful movements. This develops the pincer grasp for writing along with more advanced muscular control. Because of the advanced fine-motor coordination required, I wouldn't recommend using water beads for graphing with children who have difficulty with fine-motor

activities or are easily frustrated. It's wonderful for children who enjoy a challenge.

How to prepare the activity:
Step 1. Soak the water beads in water to hydrate them.
Step 2. Add 10 water beads of each color to a bowl of water.
Step 3. Print out the color-graph printable on white cardstock.
Step 4. Laminate the printed page. When cutting around the laminated page, leave a laminate edge of approximately ¼ inch to prevent water from reaching the cardstock.
Step 5. Place laminated printable and bowl with water beads on tray.

Activity directions for children:
1. Without looking, reach into the bowl and pick up a water bead.
2. Place the water bead above the correct color word.
3. Continue until one column reaches 10.

This can be played as a cooperative game. Two or more children can do the work together, taking turns to see which color reaches 10 first. Have fun!

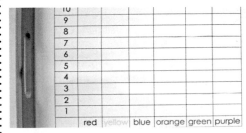

Deb Chitwood, M.A. - Living Montessori Now

Living Montessori Now

Information and Inspiration for Parents and Teachers

Deb Chitwood is a certified Montessori teacher with a master's degree in Early Childhood Studies. Deb taught in Montessori schools before becoming director of her own Montessori school. Later, she homeschooled her two children from preschool through high school. She's the author of the book Montessori at Home or School: How to Teach Grace and Courtesy and writes about Montessori activities and ideas on her blog at LivingMontessoriNow.com.

Color Mixing Explosion Experiment

Fine Motor, Sensory, Color Learning, Science, Science Experiments

Pre-school

Kinder-garten

You will need:

1 tablespoon of baking soda
White vinegar (enough to fill your cup 3/4 full)
Clear plastic cup
Bowl or other container to set cup in
Food coloring in primary colors

How to:

This is a great experiment for young children who are learning about color mixing. It is especially fun to see the excitement on their faces the first time they try it. Since we have four 4 year-old children, I had them try it out separately so that each one was surprised by the results. This would also work well in a classroom, with children working in teams doing different steps of the experiment.

Set up the experiment by placing the plastic cup inside of your larger container. Fill the cup about 3/4 full of white vinegar. Then, set two primary colors out (such as yellow and blue), on each side of the large container. Set a premeasured tablespoon of baking soda within reach near the large container. Instruct your child to add a little bit of the first color to the cup of vinegar (off to one side) and then the next color to the other side. It doesn't really matter where they place the drops of color. It is just easier for them to see the colors mixing if they place the drops on opposite sides. Finally, have your child add the tablespoon of baking soda to the cup and see what happens.

To see this experiment in action, check out the video (http://youtu.be/Sq7HUMLMKHQ) of our 4 year-old son, Grayson, trying it out for the first time. He was really amazed! Try the experiment with different color combinations, such as red and yellow or red and blue. Have your children predict what will happen when the colors mix together. There are so many fun ways for kids to learn about color mixing. If you are practicing at home, you can try color changing baths by giving your child one cup each of different colors that can be added to the bath one at a time. This can also be done in a water table in a home or school setting. Children can try adding two primary colors to shaving cream in a tray and swirling them together with a spoon. Adding an element of fun to color mixing helps them to remember it in a meaningful way.

capri +3

Multiples = Multiple Blessings

Theresa - Capri + 3

Capri + 3 is full of arts and crafts, play, science and literacy activities for children. Theresa, a psychologist, now home with her four same-age preschoolers also shares family adventures, recipes and stories of parenting multiples. http://www.multiples-mom.com/

The World Of Imagination Play

How to:

Children learn by imagining and acting. They may pretend to be Mommy, or they may crawl around the house pretending to be a puppy. There are many ways that children use role play to act out experiences.

When your child is active in imaginary play, they are developing their brain in countless ways. Research in early childhood education shows that the values of imaginary play are a vital part of the developing child.

Benefits of Imaginary Play:
Social & Emotional Skills:
When your child is engaged in pretend play, this is how they experiment with the social roles in their life. Your child wants to pretend to be a doctor and perform a checkup right before their own doctor's visit. This helps them make sense of what will happen while at the doctor, as they prepare for their own visit. This kind of play helps develop sympathy, empathy, and nurturing, as they see the world through someone else's eyes.

Language Skills:
Imaginary play helps a child understand the power of language. In order to be engaged in imaginary play, a child must have the right words to act out the story or scenario, so imaginary play allows them to come up with the words as they go along.

Problem Solving Skills:
Imaginary play allows the child to re-enact situations they see in their daily lives. How does Mommy react when we spill our cup of milk? These types of situations allow the child to solve dilemmas. By practicing problem-solving skills in imaginary situations, this will better prepare the child for solving problems in real-life situations.

Cooperative Play:
Much of the time, when a child is engaged in imaginary play, they are playing with other children. These situations require that each child takes on the role they are to play. Research shows that children are better able to control themselves and impulses more when they are engaged in imaginary play.

Encourage Imaginative Play by:
Providing a Place of Pretend
Provide your child with a place that they can pretend, but don't always restrict it to one area of the house. You don't have to feel like you are reinventing the wheel, or go out and spend a lot of money.

Provide Props
Some simple items in your home make great pretend play props. And old cardboard box provides many opportunities for a "house." Let your children play with your kitchen apron, rolling pin, or even your old cell phone!

Erica Leggiero - eLeMeNOP Kids

ELEMENO P KIDS
play. create. imagine.

Erica is a former preschool teacher with a M.Ed. in Elementary/Reading Education. She has taught children in some capacity since 2008. She firmly believes play is the way children learn. It is fun for them and they can learn about themselves, the people around them, their environments, and build skills needed for the big world! Erica is on a mission to inspire the mind, body, and spirit of your preschooler. http://www.elemenopkids.com/

pH Flowers Chemistry Art

Science, Science Experiments

Pre-school

Kinder-garten

You will need:

pH paper strips (1-14 range)
Water
Lemon juice
Baking soda
Windex or other ammonia based glass cleaner
Green pipe cleaners
Green tape (masking, washi or floral)
Cups for holding solutions
Pipettes (optional)

How to:

pH Flowers are a colorful way to create and learn with chemistry. Kids can explore the pH of some household items then use the colorful pH paper strips to create a flower bouquet. A bouquet of these flowers would make a special gift for a loved one or a favorite science teacher.

What is pH?
pH is the measure of acidity or alkalinity of a substance. It's measured on a scale from 0-14 with anything under 7 being acidic and over 7 being basic. Something right at 7 is considered to be neutral. Items you find in the house fall all over the pH scale. Citrus fruits and vinegar are acidic. Many bathroom cleaners are basic. The milk you drink is neutral.

Now let's get testing and crafting!

pH Flowers Chemistry Art Instructions
Step 1. Create solutions:
Lemon juice
½ cup water with ¼ teaspoon lemon juice
½ cup water with 1 tablespoon baking soda
Windex

Step 2. Test pH: Dip strips into each of the solutions, comparing colors. Definitely mix and play with solutions to see what pH you end up with. You can try other liquids you find around the house, too. This is a great place to talk about hypotheses... Keep dipping strips until you have enough to make your bouquet. You'll need about 5 strips per flower.

Step 3. Let strips dry: Place used test strips on a plastic tray or plate to dry keeping strips of different pH's separate or they will change color. Drying should take a couple of hours.

Step 4. Make flowers: Grab 5-6 strips between fingers in one hand, slightly fanning them out into a flower shape. Then place against the end of a pipe cleaner and wrap with tape.

Some Questions to Ask:
To keep the kids thinking during projects, I love to have some open-ended questions ready. Here are a few examples:
What pH do you think each solution will be? What colors did the strips turn? Find them on the pH paper key.
Try mixing your solutions. How did their pH change when you mixed them?
Have you ever tasted something acidic? How did it feel on your tongue?

Anne Carey - Left Brain Craft Brain

Anne, an ex-engineer and current stay-at-home mama writes about crafty ways to encourage creativity (and brain power!) in our kids. STEAM (Science / Technology / Engineering / Art / Math) projects that incorporate learning with play are her fave. http://leftbraincraftbrain.com/

ABC Scavenger Hunt

Gross Motor, Literacy, Reading, ABC

Toddler

Pre-school

Kinder-garten

You will need:

Post-it Notes or Mini Post-it Notes
Scissors
Pen or Marker
A Place to Play

How to:

Basic Prep & Game
You can use full Post-it notes, or if you want to make the most of your Post-its, cut them: If you are using mini Post-it notes take 13 of them and cut them in half so that each resulting set of notes has sticky on them. If you are using full size Post-its then you can choose to cut them in half or in thirds.

Write a letter on each post-it note, all the way through the alphabet. Next stick the post-its all around the house or play room.

Now your child can then go on an alphabet scavenger hunt! Ideally your child would look for the Post-its in order, skipping over those that come later in the alphabet but younger children may just want to grab them as they see them. Next your child would grab the letter and place it on the wall in alphabetical order and then move onto the next letter.

Game Variations & Adaptations
-You stick each letter onto something that starts with that letter (stick the letter A to an apple, B to a ball, C to the couch, etc)

and your child finds them.
-You write uppercase letters on one set of post it notes and lowercase on the other, hiding both. Your child finds them in pairs.
-With mixed age children, the older children can write and hide the letters while younger children can find them. They can use teamwork to place them in order.
-For younger children who are still working on letter recognition start by writing the same letter on several Post-its and just find those. You can do a different letter each day.
-You can also use this idea for numbers or math. Either write numbers out and find them in numerical order or write a math problem on one Post-it and the answer on another. Repeat with more math problems and hide them all.

Laura Marschel - Lalymom

Lalymom
home with two,
creativity will brew!

Laura is a Chicagoland Stay at Home Mom to two sweet redheads who fuel all the fun and creativity you find at Lalymom. You'll see fine motor skills activities, DIY toys, fun printables and more! http://lalymom.com

"It is a happy talent to know how to play."

- Ralph Waldo Emerson

Life Skills

Cooking with Kids

Kids In The Kitchen

You will need:

Children's safety knives
Spatulas
Icing spreaders (cake spatula)
Whisks
Measuring cups & spoons
Mixing bowl with a handle

How to:

We find that cooking with kids brings a lot of joy to our household. My great-nephew has been helping me in the kitchen since he was 11 months old. We enjoy cooking together and I believe I learn as much from him as he learns from me.

What are the advantages of having children help in the kitchen?
First of all, it is a great bonding time. Children love to help. It makes them feel special and "grown-up" when you let them contribute to the food preparation. A lot of learning can take place in the kitchen. When they are very young, just learning to follow directions is an important lesson. As they get older they can help by counting and later, actually learning measurements. Some children have texture issues, helping in the kitchen gives them a chance to work through those issues. You might also find that your picky eater is willing to try some different things when they are the one helping create the dish.

Safety knives for children are very handy and will allow your child to cut up fruits and vegetables. Despite the fierce look, the knives have a dull serration. My less technical term is that they have a dull "rippled" edge. Even though they aren't sharp they can cut through things like apples and cucumbers. My 3 year old great-nephew used one to help me cut up a pumpkin. Although they aren't sharp, make sure your child handles them the same way they would handle a sharp knife. Use the safety knife as a training tool. You don't want them to develop bad habits, such as grabbing the blade end of the knife. The one I have is called My Safe Cutter by Pampered Chef. I have seen another set, by a company called Curious Chef, but I haven't had the privilege of using them yet.

Icing spreaders (also called cake spatulas) are not only great for icing but they are wonderful for spreading butter and peanut butter. Their wider blade makes spreading easier than a thin bladed butter knife.

If your child is old enough to start using a hand mixer, make sure to have a mixing bowl with a handle. I was able to get the picture of my 3 year old great-nephew using a mixer, for the first time, because one hand was busy with the mixer and the other was holding the handle of the mixing bowl.

Benefits of Cooking with Kids
One benefit is sharing family history. We have many recipes that have been handed down from previous generations. Sharing those recipes and memories are precious gifts for your little ones.

For me, the top benefit of cooking with kids is the simple joy. The joy in the talking, the mess, and the laughing.

Now it's your turn for fun. Grab the kids, a mixing bowl, some ingredients and start cooking up some memories.

Mama Carmody - Love to Laugh and Learn

I was a stay-at-home mom for 13 years. All I ever wanted to be was a mother and a teacher and I have been blessed and honored to do both. Making learning fun has always been one of my main goals; whether working with my own children or with others'. Having always enjoyed writing, being able to blog about fun educational things to do with children is very rewarding. http://lovetolaughandlearn.com/

The Child-Size Home

Life Skills, Kids Helping In The Home, Chores

Toddler

Pre-school

Kinder-garten

How to:

Establishing a kid-sized home is important. It means making life a little easier for your children and it encourages their independence. It's amazing what a simple step stool can do to boost the confidence of a toddler and how happy kid-sized chair can make your little one.

The child-sized home is not hard to accomplish, but does take a little planning and rearranging. For instance, maybe you don't have the resources to build or buy a tiny kitchen cabinet, but you might be able to rearrange a lower cabinet that is specifically for all of your child's kitchen needs.

Even when helping with the chores, children should have their own supplies. This is because they can take ownership in the tasks that they are to complete and they can also take ownership in being able to be completely self sufficient. When I ask my daughter (26 months) to wipe up a spill, she has a drawer in her cabinet with towels or when there is dirt on the floor and I ask her to clean it up, she has her own hand brush, dust pan, and mini trash can. She know where they are and if it's not there, she knows that she is the one who did not put it back. So beyond being self-sufficient, it teaches responsibility in keeping track of her own things.

Creating areas throughout the home that are kid-sized can be a way for your children to feel comfortable in their own space and their own skin with the rest of the family. We created a corner with an oversized kid's chair in the living room and a children's table in the dining room. And while our older daughter does

not always use these spaces, she is very aware that they are especially for her. So when there is a meltdown over someone sitting in the recliner, we can offer that she sits in her own chair. And typically, the specialness of the chair being her own solves the problem.

Therefore, taking time to plan out the home in a kid-sized way can both help encourage independence and also help prevent melt-downs. Making the home easier to navigate with step stools, kitchen helpers, and door grips for the things that can't be changed also makes a world of difference for children of all ages.

Kara Carrero - ALLterNATIVElearning

Kara is a former classroom teacher turned mom-in-survival mode. She strives to raise eco-conscious, independent children in the modern world and enjoys every minute of this crazy life. When she's not juggling babies and toddlers, she is passionate about blogging and connecting with her readers! http://ALLterNATIVElearning.com/

Cooking with Young Children

Life Skills, Kids In The Kitchen, Kids Helping In The Home

How to:

Years ago, my friend mentioned that she did not let her son cook with her because "he wants to help me crack the eggs."

On the other hand, when my son was the same age (23 months), he would run to get his kid-sized apron, yelling "Cook! Cook!" Then, he would climb up on his stool and pound on the counter, a big smile on his face.

I am not, by any means, a fantastic cook. But I have found that expecting my children to help cook has helped them become budding cooks at a very young age, as well as encourage them to eat new things.

To include my young children in the kitchen, I try to keep their interests in mind. Sometimes I let my son choose the meal, even if I may not enjoy it. Or, I let my daughter cut a strawberry with a dull butter knife, even when I know the strawberry may end up mushed and possibly be eaten. My kids love hands on, so we make English muffin pizzas. And they definitely get to crack the eggs, even if we may have to dig out the eggshell.

Cooking with kids is definitely not a task for the weak of heart. It is messy. It is slow. It could be dangerous, so vigilance is of utmost importance. But when children are fully engaged in the most basic of family chores (preparing the food and cleaning up afterwards), they come to appreciate what they eat and they have pride in their accomplishments.

After five years of joining me in the kitchen, now my son can search through a cookbook, select a recipe, make a shopping list, do most cooking preparations, and assist with cleanup. I still help with oven and stove needs, as well as any chopping requiring our sharpest knives. My son enjoys cooking, and asks to join in whenever he gets a chance.

My young daughter also loves to be a "cooker," and begs "I do it!" as we prepare food. It's her turn for the kid-sized apron.

One of the best reasons to let a child into the kitchen is the look of delight on my toddler's face when she helps crack an egg. One minute, a hard solid service: the next, a runny gooey mess. Delighted screeches, loud laughter, and a largest smile I have seen.

That's worth any mess.

Rebecca Reid - Line upon Line Learning

Rebecca Reid is a stay-at-home homeschooling mom to two kids, "Raisin" (age 7) and "Strawberry" (age 3). She blogs on parenting, homeschooling, and life-long education at Line upon Line Learning, where she also shares supplementary educational materials for parents and teachers. http://www.lineuponlinelearning.com/

Water-Bead Pouring

Fine Motor, Life Skills

Pre-school

Kinder-garten

You will need:

Small pitcher filled with hydrated water beads and colored water for pouring
Container or containers to pour water beads into. In the photo, I used a small glass decanter and two glass oyster cups.
Small sponge for wiping up spills
Tray to hold the materials

How to:

Practical life activities are some of the most important Montessori activities because they develop order, concentration, coordination, and independence. In Montessori education, children start the practical life activities of pouring grains and beans before pouring water. Pouring trays typically start with two equal-size pitchers and progress to a tray with a pitcher and two cups before introducing a setup this difficult.

Pouring water beads isn't a traditional Montessori activity, although it uses the same techniques. It's simply a fun, more advanced variation of water pouring. Pouring water beads would be introduced after the child is comfortable pouring both dry ingredients and water.

This is how you could demonstrate water-bead pouring to a child, using slow and deliberate movements as you demonstrate.

Step 1. Carefully carry the tray from its place on the shelf to a child-size table.
Step 2. Place your right index and right middle finger through the handle of the pitcher that is on the right side of the tray.

Step 3. Place your right thumb on the top of the handle.
Step 4. Place your left index finger and left middle finger on the pitcher under the spout.
Step 5. Bring the spout of the pitcher to the center of the opening of one of the other containers.
Step 6. Tilt the pitcher slowly and watch the water beads and water pour into the container.
Step 7. When one container is filled, pour more of the water beads into another container.
Step 8. Continue until all the water beads and water have been poured into the glass containers.
Step 9. Wait until the last water bead and last drop of water have been poured.
Step 10. Return the pitcher to the upright position.
Step 11. With a similar technique, pour the water beads from each glass container back into the pitcher.
Step 12. Use the sponge to wipe the pitcher's spout and any spills.
Step 13. Replace the pouring pitcher and containers to their original spots on the tray.
Step 14. Pass the tray to the child or return the tray to the shelf.

Although pouring activities may seem overly simple, they're important in many ways. They help children develop muscular control, develop a sense of order through following a series of steps, and develop concentration when the task is repeated over and over. Children learn to clean up after themselves and become more independent. Not only can children learn to pour their own drinks, but pouring skills encourage grace and courtesy when children are able to pour a drink for someone else.

Living Montessori Now

Information and Inspiration for Parents and Teachers

Deb Chitwood, M.A. - Living Montessori Now

Deb Chitwood is a certified Montessori teacher with a master's degree in Early Childhood Studies. Deb taught in Montessori schools before becoming director of her own Montessori school. Later, she homeschooled her two children from preschool through high school. Deb is now a Montessori writer who lives in San Diego and writes about Montessori activities and ideas on her blog at LivingMontessoriNow.com.

Alphabet & Numbers Pretzel Snack

Fine Motor, Sensory, Math, Shapes, ABC, Life Skills, Kids In The Kitchen

Toddler

Pre-school

Kinder-garten

You will need:

1 packet of active dry yeast
4 cups of flour
1 1/2 cup of warm water
1 teaspoon of salt
Melted butter or 1 egg (to brush on before baking)
Coarse salt or sugar and cinnamon (optional for sprinkling on top)

How to:

One of the things that my girls and I love doing together is baking in the kitchen. The best part about cooking is that there are so many different lessons to be learned. One of our favorite recipes to make is our Pretzel Dough Recipe, in which my girls are allowed to create letters, numbers, and shapes. It's a great activity to review letters, numbers, shapes, and even sight words we have been learning. Plus, my girls are also working their fine motor skills and sensory play!

Step 1: Preheat your oven at 350 degrees.

Step 2: Mix your packet of active dry yeast, flour, and teaspoon of salt together.

Step 3: Add warm water to the bowl and mix together. We personally found that it was easier to mix with our hands rather than with a spoon. Plus it's so much more fun!

Step 4: Help your children separate the dough into small balls.

We made 12 small balls.

Step 5: Give your child a small ball of dough and ask them to make a number, letter, or shape. If you have older children allow them to create words they have learned. You could also place alphabet, number, or shape cards in front of your child so that they can visualize what they are making. This is great for younger children.

Step 6: Help your child roll out their dough into long ropes. This will make it easier when creating letters and number. Younger children might need a bit of help.

Step 7: To give your pretzel a nice golden brown finish spread some beaten egg or melted butter over the pretzels with a brush, followed with either sprinkles of sugar and cinnamon or coarse salt.

Step 8: Bake on 350 degrees for about 12-15 minutes or until pretzels are golden brown.

Step 9: If you decide to do a cinnamon and sugar pretzel add more butter on top and sprinkle with a bit of sugar and cinnamon after they are baked.

Enjoy your delicious creations!

Remember this recipe can also be made gluten free, dairy free, and egg free.

Victoria Armijo - ABC Creative Learning

ABC creative LEARNING
where ideas bloom

Hi I'm Victoria, wife and mommy of two amazing little girls! I blog over at ABC Creative Learning, where I share homeschooling ideas, kid crafts, recipes, and our love of theme parks! http://abccreativelearning.com/

Chores for Charity

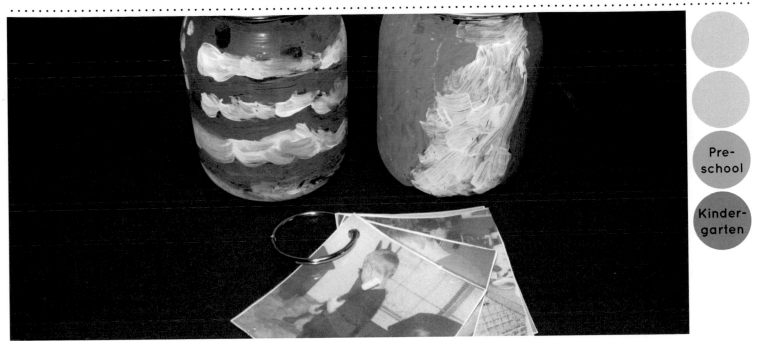

Pre-school

Kinder-garten

you will need:

Card stock
Clear contact paper
Binder ring

How to:

One Sunday at church, we heard an announcement that a children's home needed food and household supplies. My children looked at me and said, "Mom, can you give us some money so we can buy something at the store to help?"

Their question got me thinking. What are some ways they could earn their own money for giving to charities they choose?

I asked them to think of some chores that were not part of their normal routine. They could do these extra chores to earn money to give others who are in need.

We created a set of cards containing these chores so that they could choose which chores to do each time.

I took pictures of them doing each of the extra chores. My kids like to see pictures of themselves as opposed to stock pictures I find online. I used a computer program to make the pictures smaller, and fit three pictures on one page of card stock. I used Microsoft Word, but you can use other programs as well. I printed the pictures on card stock and cut them out.

*If you don't want to print your own have the pictures printed at a photo store.

I laminated the cards. My favorite way to laminate is by covering with clear contact paper. I punched a hole in the side of each card and used a big ring to keep the cards together. This makes it easier for the kids to hold onto the cards.

I placed the cards on a hook in the kitchen. Now whenever my children want to earn extra money to give to others, they can choose one from our collection.

My kids decided to decorate a special container for each of them to keep his donation money. We decorated jelly jars but you can also decorate boxes or any number of things. Use your imagination and have fun creating your donation jar!

My kids are now on the lookout for needs within our church and the community. Since they are making their own money and saving it to help others, they now have a greater sense of responsibility.

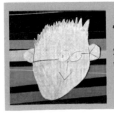
Sharla Orren - Look At What You Are Seeing

Sharla Orren loves homeschooling her two boys at her cozy homestead by the woods. She has been married to her wonderful husband for fifteen years. You can find her blogging at http://www.lookatwhatyouareseeing.com

Companion Planting Gardens

Science, Life Skills

Pre-school

Kinder-garten

You will need:

Variety of containers & Compost or soil
Stones, broken pots or tiles for drainage
Seeds or seedlings & Water
Paper and pencils for planning the gardens

How to:

What is Companion Planting?

Companion planting is where you put certain plants together when you plan out your crop garden. This means that the plants help each other by either making the garden pests go away or attract other useful bugs to the garden to eat the pests. Another way of companion planting is to provide a plant that is much tastier to the pests than the ones you are trying to grow which means that they will eat that plant rather than your crops!

Why use Companion Planting?

This method of planting is ideal for growing plants organically or with as few chemicals as possible. It is a great way to teach children that there are other methods of planting that they can use. It is also better for the useful bugs such as bees, hoverflies and ladybugs.

Getting Started;

We talked about the crop plants that we like to eat and use in the kitchen and made some drawings for a list of things we would like to grow: Carrots, Potatoes, Tomatoes, Corn. We found out that many of the herbs we were going to plant in our herb garden would actually make good companion plants

so we got our seed packets and matched them up with their companions and took photographs to refer to later. After checking online that these would work in our climate (northern UK) we set to work planning our mini crop gardens.

We matched:

Carrots with Chives – carrot pests do not like the smell of chives and chive pests do not like the smell of carrots. The wispy carrot heads plus the flowers would look great with the purple chive flowers too!
Potatoes and Horseradish – horseradish increases the disease resistance of the potatoes.
Tomatoes and Basil – the basil makes flies and mosquitos stay away. It also attracts butterflies and can make the tomatoes taste nicer too!
Once we had our companion worked out we also had to look at the plants which did not work well together!

Potatoes and tomatoes can get the same blight so need to be kept apart. We also knew that scented marigolds are very good for planting too. The smell drives away many pests however slugs love them. This means that you can use them to attract the slugs AWAY from your crop plants!

So we have three containers that will be planted with our companion plants and we have smaller containers to be put around with marigolds in. Once you start exploring companion planting it becomes fascinating way of gardening that is eco-friendly and produces great food crops. Plus it can be an interesting way of growing things together that can also look beautiful too!

Helen - Witty Hoots

Helen Newberry is a teacher, art historian and business woman. Juggling a home, career and family, including a 13 year gap between her two children, means she is constantly striving to make Witty Hoots a useful resource for busy families. http://wittyhoots.com/

Daily & Nightly Routine Posters

Life Skills, Kids Helping In The Home, Chores

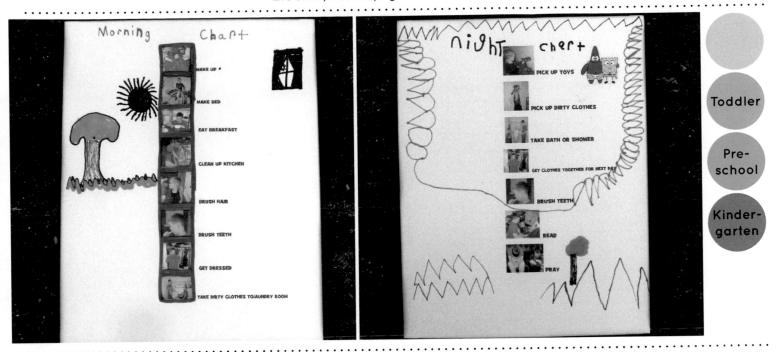

Toddler

Pre-school

Kinder-garten

You will need:

Card stock
Color markers
Cheap document frames
Stickers

How to:

Having daily and nightly routines posted so your children can see them is a helpful way for them to know what is expected of them. It also helps them to form good organizational habits while they are young. I started posting simple routines for my children when they were toddlers. Now that they are 7 and 11, the expectations for them have grown; but the routines still help them visualize their routine.

Here are some benefits for posting daily and nightly routines.
- Posting routines helps your children know what is expected of them each day and night.
- Posting routines helps your children learn to do things by themselves.
- Posting routines helps your children turn new chores into natural habits. This can reduce whining.
- Posting routines helps your children do things more quickly and with less fussing.
- Posting routines helps create more peaceful mornings since those mornings are prepared for the night before.
- Posting routines helps you be more consistent and focused.

Making creative and eye catching posters for theses routines is easy and fun.

How to make the posters:

Step 1. List what you would like your children to accomplish. Make a morning list and a night list. Include "normal" things, such as brushing teeth; chores, such as taking clothes to the laundry; and fun things, such as reading.
Step 2. Take pictures of your children doing the created routine. You can also use stock pictures that you find online, or even let them draw their own pictures.
Step 3. Print your day and night routines on card stock. Remember to separate the morning routine from the night routine. I use the 8 ½ X 11 sized card stock.
Step 4. Let your kids decorate their new posters. They can use markers, stickers, colors, or whatever is available. Let them be creative!
Step 5. Place each poster in a frame and hang them where your kids can easily see them. Feel free to use inexpensive document frames. After all, the posters are already decorated.

I have included some templates for you to use if you wish. If this is your first time posting routines, work with your children several times until they can do it themselves. It may seem like a lot of work at first; but, as your children grow you will see it was well worth the time and effort.

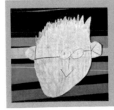

Sharla Orren - Look At What You Are Seeing

Sharla Orren loves homeschooling her two boys at her cozy homestead by the woods. She has been married to her wonderful husband for fifteen years. http://www.lookatwhatyouareseeing.com/

"Play is often talked about as if it were a relief from serious learning. But for children play is serious learning. Play is really the work of childhood."

– Fred Rogers

Organization and Setup of Play / Reading / Explore Areas

Organize Montessori Materials

Baby

Toddler

Pre-school

Kinder-garten

How to:

Montessori materials are some of the most beautiful and used materials in our home. We have lots of great handmade materials along with traditional materials. Where to store all the materials is a challenge. I want to share some of my favorite techniques to organize Montessori materials.

Photo boxes are great and can be labeled. Labels help me know what I put in a box. I also have index cards I tape to the front of boxes to easily change out the label if the box becomes repurposed.

Clear bins are my favorite. Most of my bins were on sale. We have shoe box sizes all the way up to large bins. They are a great quick way to see in each bin and to organize.

The best set of shelves in our home are adjustable metal shelves. They are easy to break down for a move and fit nicely in small spaces. Shelves allow you to use vertical space.

Baskets and trays are a huge part of Montessori education. We stack them inside one another and store them on top of cabinets and under beds. We have a large basket designated as the basket for baskets!

A great way to organize Montessori materials is by themes. We have many themed boxes for holidays or special events like our study on seeds.

I am a huge fan of vertical space. The shelf above was a free

shelf I saved from the trash made of heavy wood. In our one bedroom apartment, the bottom shelves are practical life, but the top shelves, including the very top, are all storage.

The use of clear bins and the vertical space made this a practical area in our home.

Not everyone has huge closets to dedicate to organize their Montessori materials so I want to share some of my secret spaces to store items. Under the bed, we have clear bins with labels. Books are great to store under the bed because they can be too heavy for weak shelving. Another secret space is on top of the cabinets in the kitchen. We store our baskets on the top of the cabinets in decorative baskets. Another secret space is to add a shelf above the hanging clothes in a closet to add a lot of extra storage space.

I love all of our Montessori materials and keeping them organized helps them last longer. Also, organizing helps busy Mommas find what they need quickly.

Marie Mack- Child Led Life

Marie is an educator (and former Black Hawk pilot) turned work-at-home mom who blogs about her family's adventures in a child led life at ChildLedLife.com. She shares fun activities for kids, parenting tips, help with homeschool setup, great product reviews, and more. http://childledlife.com/

Simple Toy And Book Storage Idea

Baby

Toddler

Pre-school

Kinder-garten

you will need:

Over-the-door shoe organizer
Seam ripper
Needle and thread

How to:

Placing books in over-the-door storage is a great way to save space. Shoe organizers are convenient for storing many things, with their multiple compartments, however they are often too small for books. This tutorial teaches you how to neatly combine some of the compartments to hold larger books as well.

A cheap over-the-door shoe hanger works best for this. Look for one that has a line of stitching separating the various pockets on the front. I used a cheap vinyl over-the-door rack in black from IKEA.

Step 1. Work from the back of the organizer. Find the stitching that separates two sections and carefully tear it open with a seam ripper. Your two sections are now one. However, as you see, it hangs open too much to contain anything.
Step 2. Switch to the front of the shoe rack. You will see that removing the seam has formed a pleat. Find the outer corners of the top of the pleat, and sew together with a few simple in-and-out stitches.

Step 3. Repeat with as many compartments as you'd like. However, do it in sets of two. Combining more than two sections will not work, unless you take it in with new seams along the

way, as it hangs open too much.

Step 4 (optional). Decorate with puffy paint, fabric markers, or trim it with duct tape. You can involve the children in this stage - they will love it! Try downloading stencils and painting on the alphabet, or images that represent what each section is for.

I've kept some sections smaller to hold the various parts of shape sorters, stacking cups, and similar toys. I've expanded some to fit stuffed animals as well. It's a great way to store craft supplies and other items, while allowing you the flexibility of having larger compartments.

It's easy as that!

Menucha - Moms & Crafters

Hi! I'm Menucha, the lone force behind Moms and Crafters. I'm a mom to a mischievous little toddler, freelance graphic designer, jewelry artist, and chocolate lover! I blog full time, and craft in my spare time.
http://momsandcrafters.com/

Making Book Baskets

Toddler

Pre-school

Kinder-garten

How to:

We have a lot of books, and it can sometimes be hard to focus on a particular kind of book or even to find the books on a certain subject when we want or need them. My daughter is very into space, for example, and when she wants to read one of her space books it's good to have them as close to hand as possible.

I started making book baskets to help keep like books together and to serve as a way to consciously rotate books so we might read more of our collection more often.

You book basket can be based on anything you want or whatever your child is interested in.

Some ideas include:
- Holidays and seasons
- A particular animal or kinds of animals (jungle animals, sea life)
- Space
- Art
- Dance
- Music
- A particular character your child likes
- Books about feelings or something your child is going through (visits to the doctor, starting school)
- Whatever your child is interested in

How to Make a Book Basket
I have a sturdy rubber tub that I use for my book basket. It's attractive and easy to carry, which is nice.

I like to include five or more books on a particular theme, but however many you have is great. You can also take a trip to the library to find books on your subject. These can be picture books, solid nonfiction reference books, easy readers, chapter books, whatever you think your child is ready for and will be interested in.

I usually include some extras to make it a little more fun. For example the winter basket had a knit penguin and the space basket includes a notebook and pen for recording observations, an LED flashlight and some printouts of the planet shapes. These things can help draw the child to the basket if they're a reluctant reader, and they give antsy kids something to do while you read to them.

Rotating Book Baskets
Like toy rotation, there's a bit of an art to rotating books through the basket. You want to leave the books there while your child is enjoying them, but not so long that they stop going to the basket. A couple of weeks to a month is probably enough time between baskets, and it makes it fun (for them and for you) if it's changed regularly.

After doing this for a while your child may offer suggestions for book baskets or start to make their own (my daughter calls them her "quiet time" baskets, though she doesn't always use them for that).

Book baskets are a fun and easy way to encourage reading, to be able to talk about how different authors look at similar subjects, and to learn more about things your child is interested in. And if you leave it in a conspicuous place it shows literally that books play a central role in family life, which is a great lesson at any age.

Sarah E. White - Our Daily Craft

Our Daily Craft
Sarah E. White is a crafter, writer, knitwear designer and mom living in Arkansas. She writes about crafting with and for children, creativity for moms and other busy people and creating the life you always wanted at Our Daily Craft. She also writes for the knitting websites at About.com and Craftgossip.com and is the author of three knitting books. http://ourdailycraft.com/

Organizing Loose Parts For Outdoors

Toddler

Pre-school

Kinder-garten

you will need:

Miscellaneous loose parts
Easy-open waterproof containers

How to:

Pediatricians across the country are crying out about how the excess of screen time is harming children's eyes and how the excess of sitting around the house is causing an obesity epidemic among our youth.

Child psychiatrists across the nation are warning us of a drastic increase in children who feel stressed out, depressed, anxious and generally just unhappy. The experts agree that these problems are all caused by a lack of playtime outside.

Parents often say, "I'd love to take my kid outside every day but they get so bored and I just don't have the money for a bunch of toys that will get left out in the rain."
You don't have to spend money on outdoor toys for kids. You can pull off fun activities and play outside every day with what you have on hand already; you just don't know it yet.

The trick to getting kids to play outside more is simple: open-ended play.

Play that is not directed. Play that is whatever they want to make of it.

The best way to do that is offer them loose parts to play with.

Loose parts are anything you can give your child that is safe for them to play with. Don't worry about how they'll use it, they'll find ways of using it that you couldn't even dream of.

Examples of loose parts include but are not limited to:
- acorns
- beads (plastic, glass, or wooden)
- bottle caps
- cheap plastic toys (think stuff that comes in party favor bags)
- dice
- dry beans (kids love to plant these, dig them up, and plant them again)
- feathers
- game pieces from old or broken games (Boggle cubes, scrabble tiles, Monopoly houses, etc.)
- glass gems
- rocks (collect colorful ones when you see them at the park)
- sea shells (find them at the beach or use the leftovers from a summer craft project)
- seed pods
- silk flowers or leaves

Basically just look at what you have on hand already and use that! Do the same when organizing loose parts. You could go to the dollar store and buy several nice plastic containers to store your loose parts in, but I recommend reusing your old food containers instead. Make use of that empty peanut butter jar, that bottle of spaghetti sauce, that tub of butter.

Caitlyn "Suzy" Stock - Suzy Homeschooler

Caitlyn is a geeky mom of two who writes about homeschooling ideas, activities, and lesson plans.
http://suzyhomeschooler.com/

Sensory Wall Mosaic Art

Fine Motor, Sensory, Gross Motor, Color Learning, Math, Shapes, Organization And Setup Of Play / Reading / Explore Areas

- Baby
- Toddler
- Pre-school
- Kinder-garten

You will need:

Contact paper
Pattern blocks or foam blocks
Painter tape

How to:

Following the huge success of our pattern blocks on contact paper play, I decided to try putting it all up on our wall using painters tape. Emma helped me place several feet of contact paper, and the kids and I had a blast using pattern blocks to create mosaics on our dining room wall!

The wooden blocks make for an incredible visual and sensory experience! We decided to add in some small foam blocks we had.

These were easier for the kids to stick on, since they are lighter weight – you have to press the pattern blocks on for them to stay – but once up, they'll stay for hours (it's been over 48 hours now, and they've remained stuck to our wall without any trouble). At first, I worried that the contact paper might ruin the wooden blocks, but it doesn't seem to be causing any trouble.

Johnny especially loved the feel of the soft foam stuck to the contact paper – all the more since we had the blocks spelling out his and Emma's names!

We left this up for several days, and the kids enjoyed admiring it and occasionally moving pieces around. We have repeated the experience on rainy days and with friends, and it is always a hit!

mama smile

MaryAnne - Mama Smiles

Mama Smiles
JOYFUL PARENTING

An educator and researcher turned mother raising four children (born 2006, 2007, 2009, and 2012) in Silicon Valley, California, MaryAnne blogs about crafts, outings, and educational activities that her family enjoys. She loves to promote ways families can learn, play, and create together. MaryAnne has a Masters degree in education and a Ph.D. In medicine (public health). http://www.mamasmiles.com/

Tips To Organize Art Supplies

Organization And Setup Of Play / Reading / Explore Areas

Toddler

Pre-school

Kinder-garten

How to:

As an art teacher, I have always wanted my children to feel free to make art whenever they feel like it. If we had to clear off tables and track down supplies every time my daughters want to make something, we would miss out on a lot of creative time just because it's such a hassle! To combat this, we created a "Creativity Corner" just for making art, and now it is so easy to grab art supplies and create!

There are a couple of key elements, many of which I learned through trial and error as an elementary art teacher.

- All things must have a set place where they always go. Without that, things get chaotic quickly.
- Everything should be kept in easy-to-carry containers to make it easy to take things out and then put away.
- Put like things together. If my daughter wants to do watercolors, she can grab the watercolor box which has watercolors, brushes, and water cups.
- Things must be easily grabbed by little hands. Those hanging cups on the bar (Ikea) are perfect for this. My five-year-old daughter can easily reach the cups, but they are just out of reach of the two-year-old who is a little too young for free access to scissors and glue! We keep the most frequently used materials in the cups--pens/pencils, colored pencils, markers, glue/scissors, dry erase markers, and do-a-dot painters.
- Having a dedicated box for paper scraps is so important, because it saves cleaning time and allows kids to save that extremely important piece of paper that kind of looks like an elephant without you losing your mind with paper bits all over the house.

- Don't forget to have a place to store finished artworks. I have a box for artwork that has been taken down from the fridge/walls that you can't bring yourself to throw away, but it doesn't get stuck in piles of mail, mixed in with clean paper, or tossed on the floor or in the toy box (or does this only happen at my house?).

Since we created our Creativity Corner last year, I have noticed my five-year-old draws and creates way more than she used to. She has ownership over the space, freedom to implement any idea she imagines, and our house is now filled with drawings, collages, and colorful paintings!

Cindy Ingram - The Art Curator for Kids

Cindy Ingram was once an art teacher and museum educator with an MA in Art Education, and is now a work-at-home mom of two lovely daughters (ages 3 and 5). She is passionate about the power of art in people's lives and writes about how to teach art appreciation and enjoy art history with kids of all ages at The Art Curator for Kids. http://artcuratorforkids.com/

Set Up Play For Groups & Mixed Ages

Baby

Toddler

Pre-school

Kinder-garten

You will need:

No required materials; classic open-ended toys are recommended.

How to:

Playing in groups, particularly groups with mixed ages and abilities, is a wonderful learning experience for children! Older kids develop leadership skills, while younger children are introduced to new ideas and benefit from seeing higher order play modeled by children who are a little older than themselves. The built-in range of abilities that you find in any group teaches children about empathy while building social and emotional intelligence. Playing together is a wonderful way to build lifelong sibling bonds.

Here are some easy ways to help children get started playing in groups:

GET OUTDOORS
Nature is a great equalizer. Being outdoors together can spark wonderful creative play, and children learn easily in nature. Older kids see the world through new eyes thanks to their younger, shorter friends and siblings.

MAKE SPACE
Children need some space to play together in a group. The amount of space is less important than having uncluttered space. Find a part of your home where children can sit together that also has nice natural light. In our home, the master

bedroom had the best natural light, so we moved our bed to a smaller room and made that room the playroom. The play that this arrangement has inspired is well worth losing the master suite.

CHOOSE OPEN-ENDED TOYS
Open-ended toys encourage creative play, and creative play encourages cooperation between children. Here are a few open-ended toys that all four of my children (aged 2 to 9 years old) enjoy:

* Wooden blocks
* LEGO DUPLO bricks
* Magna-Tiles
* Felt boards
* Puzzles
* Dolls
* Stuffed animals
* Play silks

Getting creative is also a wonderful way for groups of kids to play together! Here are some of our favorite creative activities:

Drawing & Coloring
Painting & Play Dough
Building with and decorating cardboard boxes
Sidewalk chalk (outside)

Classic, open-ended toys are a bit of an investment, but in our home they have been well worth the investment. My four children play together for hours, and my friends' children and my nieces and nephews LOVE coming to our home! The kids disappear to play, and the adults can visit. It's a win for everyone!

MaryAnne - Mama Smiles

An educator and researcher turned mother raising four children (born 2006, 2007, 2009, and 2012) in Silicon Valley, California, MaryAnne blogs about crafts, outings, and educational activities that her family enjoys. She loves to promote ways families can learn, play, and create together. MaryAnne has a Masters degree in education and a Ph.D. in medicine. http://www.mamasmiles.com/

The Perfect Book Nook

Baby

Toddler

Pre-school

Kinder-garten

you will need:

Pillows
Rugs
Baskets
Books
Magazines

How to:

Designing your reading space can be simple and easy. Start by clearing out a space that is free of foot traffic and away from loud areas in your home or classroom. I love to start by completely clearing out the area I plan to design in and slowly adding the features. Another great feature to think about when designing a reading space is natural light. How can you best utilize the walls, the corners, and the natural boundaries of the space? All of these features will help you later when you curate the materials and plan for your invitations to learn.

In order to help children focus on the purpose and intent of the space, you want to think about rotating your books and materials and keeping minimal materials out at a time. Starting with a fresh slate will help you de-clutter and focus your attention on how you want the space to be used.

Making a reading space inviting has two parts: 1) you need your children to WANT to come to this area and stay awhile. You need them to be comfortable and the materials interesting to them. 2) You need the learning to be an invitation. You need the environment to tell the children how to use the space without the assistance of an adult.

No matter how much thought and planning you put into a reading space, it doesn't automatically mean a child will know how to use the space. You could find yourself frustrated and feeling like all of it was not worth your time. It is incredibly important to scaffold the area so that all of the children can use the area; however it is okay to strategically model how to use some or all of the materials.

Dayna Abraham - Lemon Lime Adventures

Dayna is a National Board Certified teacher with over 12 years of experience in the primary classroom. She recently began homeschooling her 3 children against her will. She writes at Lemon Lime Adventures, where she writes about the trials, successes and errors of their life, life living as a blended family, and dealing with a son with Sensory Processing Disorder. http://www.lemonlimeadventures.com

"The things he sees are not just remembered; they form a part of his soul."

- Maria Montessori

Seasonal / Holiday

Valentines Color Sorting and Counting

Color Learning, Math, Counting

Pre-school

Printable

You will need:

Foam hearts (red, orange, yellow, green, blue, and purple)
Colored hearts printable

How to:

This simple color and counting activity can be done with one child or with a small group of children, at home or in a preschool setting. While it is designed for Valentines day, it can be done throughout the year.

Putting this activity together is easy! Simply download and print enough copies of the colored heart printable for each child that will be participating. Divide the foam hearts so that each child gets at least five of each color. Make sure they are mixed up in one container, not yet sorted.

To start, have the children sort the hearts by color on a flat surface. Ask them what the names of the colors are. Then, have them take one foam heart of each color and place it on the matching color on the printable. Have them continue adding foam hearts to the matching hearts on the printable until all have been used.

Here are some ways to extend this activity:

What doesn't belong? - After the children place the foam hearts on the matching colored hearts on the printable, have them cover their eyes. Mix some of the hearts up and have them identify which ones have been moved, and then place them on matching hearts.

How many? - Remove all foam hearts from the printable. Ask the children to place three blue foam hearts on the matching paper heart. Continue to do this with the other colors, changing the amount.

Simple addition and subtraction - After placing a certain amount of foam hearts on the printable hearts, have them add one more. How many are on the heart now? Then, remove one. How many are on the heart? You can add more of a challenge depending on how high of a number you go.

Swapping hearts - if multiple children are involved, have them swap hearts with each other. One child can ask another child for two red hearts (or whatever color and number they choose). This is an excellent way to build those communication skills, too!

Sheryl Cooper - Teaching 2 and 3 Year Olds

Sheryl has been an early childhood educator for over 15 years, teaching 2 and 3 year olds in a small private preschool. She shares ideas on her blog for teachers, parents, and anyone who has young children in their lives. http://www.teaching2and3yearolds.com/

Valentines Sensory Box

Fine Motor, Sensory, Imagination Play, Color Learning, Counting

Toddler

Pre-school

Kinder-garten

you will need:

Container - under bed storage box/roasting dish/washing up bowl
Rice
Red food colouring - You can also use pink/purple or leave the rice white
Utensils
Hearts
Flowers
Small containers
Pipe cleaners
Straws
Cookie cutters
Ribbons
Any other items of your choice

How to:

Step 1. Colour your rice.
Pour the rice into a container and begin to add the food coloring. Use a metal spoon to work the color through the rice. Adding more food coloring will create darker shades. Once you are happy, leave it to dry.

Step 2. Think of some interesting items you can add to the box. I have mentioned some above. You will find you have lots of items already in your house that you can add to create different sensory experiences and textures. You may want to purchase some new items to add too.

Step 3. Decorate the set up ready to be explored and create your invitation to play. Leave the activity out and wait until your child/children come over to take a closer look.

Play time!

Note: Due to small parts always make sure you closely supervise.

Amy Powell - Learning and Exploring Through Play

Learning & Exploring Through Play
Inspiring Ideas for Little Learners

Amy is a stay-at-home mom with a background in education. She is passionate about children learning through their play and that is the driving force behind her blog. Learning and Exploring Through Play is full of inspiring arts, crafts and sensory play ideas for children. http://learningandexploringthroughplay.com/

Do-a-dot Marker Heart Card

Pre-school

You will need:

Pink cardstock 6×12 inches folded in half
Dot markers
Scissors
Cardboard
Markers
Heart stamps

How to:

Remember when you were a child in grade school, making your first Valentine's Day card for a classmate? You really wanted it to be special. Send a simple, heartfelt message with this sweet and oh-so-easy handmade Valentine's Day cards which says " You color my world."

• Cut out a large heart shape from a cardboard. This will be our stencil.
• Place the stencil in the middle of your 6×6 cardstock card. Dab the centre of the stencil with yellow dots. Use a red dot marker along the border.
• Dab the dot markers over the card and watch the colours blend together. The markers produce an effect similar to water colour paint and are great for exploring colour recognition and patterns.
• Have the kids gently dab the marker, otherwise the colors will bleed.
• Wait for it to dry and then carefully lift the stencil.

We added "Valentine, You Colour My World!" on the card.
Use it as a card or as a gift tag with homemade heart shaped crayons inside.

These colourful cards are simple to make and a great way to explore colours. Chunky dot markers are perfect for little hands to grab and use.

Shruti - Artsy Craftsy Mom

Artsy Craftsy Mom

Shruti Bhat wears many hats throughout her day - Mum to lil p, wife, friend, a quality analyst at work and the chief dreamer at ArtsyCraftsyMom where she shares creative mum-tested ideas for children and their parents.
http://artsycraftsymom.com/

Sweetheart Straw Toppers

Fine Motor

Toddler

Pre-school

Kinder-garten

You will need:

Paper straws
Card stock or scrapbook paper
Glue dots
Scissors

How to:

It's not the weekend visits to play museums or the grand vacation you could barely afford that children will remember. Rather, it's the everyday moments—the warm bedtime snuggles, the feeling in his tummy as you push him higher on the swing, the conversations and laughter at dinner—that children will recall fondly as they grow. Kids are naturally delighted by simplicity, and Valentine's Day is the perfect holiday for small gestures of love and appreciation.

Sweetheart Straw Toppers are not expensive or time consuming to make, but they are guaranteed to bring on the smiles.

1. Use scissors to cut out a paper heart.
2. Place a glue dot near the top of the straw.
3. Press the heart onto the glue dot.
4. Repeat directions 1-3 until you've reached the desired quantity of straw toppers.

Make several straw toppers at once and keep them on hand to bring a little sweetness to snack time, any time!

Melissa Lennig - Fireflies and Mud Pies

Fireflies + Mud Pies

Melissa Lennig is the voice behind Fireflies and Mud Pies, a children's activity blog that is packed with inexpensive activities and crafts to encourage families to play, create, and celebrate childhood. Social-emotional growth, nature crafts, outdoor play, and "from scratch" cooking are just a few of her passions. Melissa shares creative, low-cost ideas for learning, connecting, and playing at home. http://www.firefliesandmudpies.com/

Weaving Hearts

Fine Motor

Pre-school

Kinder-garten

You will need:

1 heart (cut from a foam sheet)
4 thin strips of foam sheet

How to:

Weaving is a wonderful way to practice fine motor skills with preschoolers and kindergarteners. It is also a great way for children to learn how to create patterns and to work through problems they may encounter while weaving. Weaving can be done with very few materials and with little set up. It is a great activity for keeping kids busy for a long period of time. This weaving activity I am sharing with you is perfect for Valentine's Day because it is uses foam hearts.

To set up this activity, cut out a large heart from a foam sheet. This heart will be the "loom" for this weaving activity. Next, cut four thin strips from a different color foam sheet. Use a pencil to make marks on the foam heart so you know where to make the slits. You will have four rows of slits. The first three rows will have four slits and the last row will only have two slits. After you've made the markings with the pencil, make the slits using a knife or X-acto knife.

After your heart is set up, invite the child to weave the four thin strips of foam through the heart. Show them how to make a pattern with going over and under for the weave. After all the strips are weaved through the heart, cut off the ends that are sticking off the sides of the heart.

This activity is simple, yet a powerful way to practice fine motor skills. If your child has difficulty weaving with the heart, try using a larger heart. If the activity is too easy, try the activity with a smaller heart or use a different material such as yarn, ribbon, or paper. After you create these weaving hearts, you'll love how colorful and festive they are for Valentine's Day.

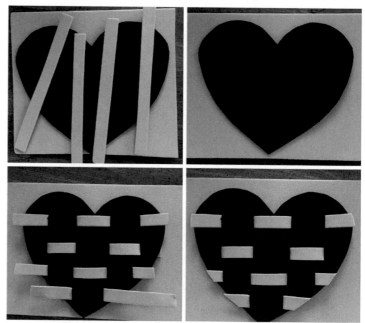

Angela Thayer - Teaching Mama

Teaching Mama

playing, creating, and learning at home

Angela is a wife to an amazing man, mama to three boys, lover of the Midwest, and daughter of Christ. She is a former teacher, turned stay-at-home mom. She loves creating fun and educational activities for her children and sharing her ideas on the blog, Teaching Mama. http://teachingmama.org/

Footprint Race Car Card

Fine Motor

Baby

Toddler

Pre-school

Kinder-garten

You will need:

Paint
Construction paper
Glue stick
Glitter glue
Permanent marker
Card stock or canvas
And some little feet!

How to:

One of our favorite ways to make our own Valentine's Day cards is using handprint or footprint art. It's the perfect craft for toddlers and preschoolers, and makes the perfect keepsake! That is why I'm sharing one of our favorites an easy footprint race car card that can be made to make the perfect Valentine or even a Mother's Day or Father's Day card. Or add the prints to a canvas to create an adorable holiday keepsake!

To start the race car footprint, your child will first choose the color that they'd like the car and then you can paint their foot, or depending on the child's age they can do this step themselves. Because it took a few times for me to get a good footprint, we did a few on a separate piece of card stock and then cut out the print that turned out the best leaving a small trim of paper around the print. Next your child can add in a fun racing stripe or any other decorations using some glitter glue.

The wheels, helmet, and any other decorations for the car can be done by using construction paper. Cut out your shapes for

the wheels and helmet and then glue them onto the car. If this is going to be used as a Valentine's Day card take a black marker and add in a fun saying like "You Make My Heart Race!" or " I Wheelie Like You, Valentine!". However, if you choose to do this activity as a keepsake, add this to a canvas and be sure to put your child's name and date on the back.

You make my heart race!

Jackie Houston - I Heart Arts n Crafts

Jackie is a stay-at-home mom who writes over at I Heart Arts n Crafts. Where she shares her latest adventures in mommyhood from free printables, parenting advice while surviving the terrible twos and her favorite arts & crafts projects! http://www.iheartartsncrafts.com/

Frozen, Fizzy Baking Soda Hearts

Fine Motor, Sensory, Play Recipes, Science Experiments

Pre-school

Kinder-garten

You will need:

Heart mold tray or heart-shaped foil cupcake liners
Box baking soda
2 cups vinegar
Mini-basters
Large container that can get messy!
Optional: food colouring

How to:

This fizzy baking soda hearts science experiment is a great, fun introduction to chemistry – perfect for Valentine's Day!

If you've never done a vinegar and baking soda experiment, you're in for a treat! Make sure to have extra hearts on hand, because the kids will beg for more!

If you've already done vinegar and baking soda experiments, now might be the time to introduce your children to the concept of a science experiment and the different steps involved (called the scientific method), which we will outline below.

First, to make the baking soda hearts, mix a generous amount of baking soda with just enough water to make it into a paste. I added some red food dye to the water before making the paste, but that's optional.

I prefer using my silicone muffin pan, or you could alternatively fill in some cookie cutters on a parchment paper-lined tray.

Freeze the baking soda hearts for two hours or overnight.

In the meantime, find a container that can get messy! I had four big kids and our "junior big kid" doing this preschool science experiment, so I used the container that we used to use for an impromptu sandbox.

I set up four small baby food jars with a quarter cup of vinegar each – I should have added at least half a cup as I had to add extra in during the experiment – and added some great mini basters to each jar.

Get the frozen hearts out of the freezer, give one to each child and show them how to squeeze the vinegar into the baster, and then wait until their baster is over the heart before squeezing the vinegar out.

I love that this is at once a science experiment – teaching wonder, process, and patience – while being a fun sensory experience (touching and watching the fizzy hearts) and a practical life opportunity, with the children learning how to use a baster.

Each heart took about 20 minutes to fully dissolve, but the kids loved every minute of it! The one heart that we allowed to get to room temperature dissolved much quicker, which prompted some interesting conclusions:
• the ice protected the baking soda
• the vinegar melted both the ice and baking soda
• vinegar is slow on cold things

If you're going to take the opportunity to teach the kids the basic foundation of the scientific method, gather them together before you get the hearts out of the freezer, or just have one heart on hand to show them.

1. Ask a Question
Tell them what you've made and ask them what they think is going to happen when you squirt vinegar on the frozen baking soda hearts.
2. Do Background Research
Encourage them to remember their past experiments.
3. Construct a Hypothesis
What do they think will happen? This may sound odd, but my kids love to start sentences with, "My hypothesis is…" It's something that they learned from Dinosaur Train and I think they really enjoy being able to have a way to express their ideas in a profound way.
4. Test your Hypothesis by Doing an Experiment
Do the experiment, encourage them to make observations throughout – what do they see happening?
5. Analyze Data and Draw a Conclusion
Have them discuss what they observed and help them look up extra information online if they have additional questions about why something happened.
6. Communicate Results
Have your child communicate or document their experiment's results in the way that they are most interested. Allow them to perform, draw, write – whatever method of communication they need to use at the time.

Jennifer Tammy - Study at Home Mama

Jennifer Tammy is a Canadian Psychologist currently at home with her daughter, running a full-time Montessori daycare. She loves sharing parenting inspiration and hands-on learning ideas on her blogs!
http://studyathomemama.ca/

Button Heart Cards

Fine Motor, Shapes

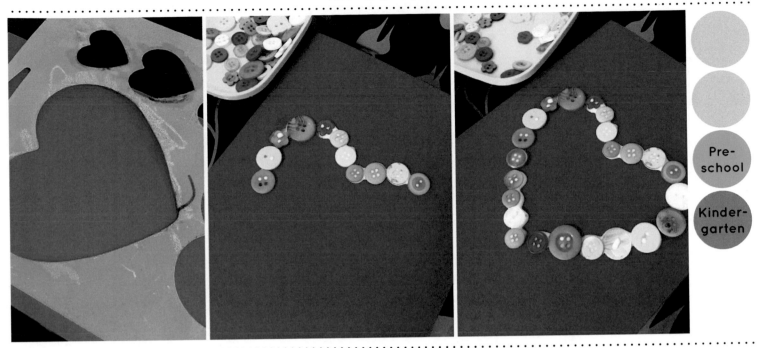

you will need:

One pre-folded card in your chosen colour
A collection of small buttons in colours that complement your main card colour
White craft glue
A pencil
A large, heart-shaped craft stencil*

How to:

My daughter loves to create handmade cards for friends and family members and so I am always on the lookout for simple-to-make card ideas. This cute button heart card makes a lovely, thoughtful gift for Valentine's Day and for birthdays and it is super adaptable too, just swap out the shape you are using to give your card a completely different look and feel – a star filled with bright yellow or gold buttons or the initial letter of the gift recipient's name in their favourite colours – just two of so many possibilities!

The card is easy enough for a preschooler or kindergartener to make pretty much independently, they will just need a little verbal guidance from you as they work through each of the following steps.

To make a button heart card, have your child:
Step 1. Trace around the heart-shaped stencil with pencil on the front of the pre-folded card.

*If you don't have a stencil, you can most definitely draw your shape freehand or trace around a large cookie cutter or other household object.

Step 2. Begin gluing buttons into place with the craft glue. To help define the shape, start by gluing buttons just inside the shape you have drawn, following the edge of your shape.

Step 3. Once the outline is complete, fill the inside of the shape with buttons too.

Step 4. Set aside until the glue has dried and then add your special Valentine or birthday message.

Christie Burnett - Childhood 101

Christie Burnett is the mum of two, early childhood teacher, author and blogger behind the playful online space known as Childhood 101. She is passionate about children's play, creativity and learning, and tries hard to prioritise time for family in the busyness of every day life. At Childhood101.com you'll find playful activity and project ideas for kids, family friendly recipes, ideas for family fun and positive parenting reflections. http://childhood101.com/

Heart Name Game

Fine Motor, Reading, Writing, Learning To Write My Name, ABC

Pre-school

Kinder-garten

You will need:

Colored card stock
Scissors
Markers

How to:

Educator Carol Lyons has said, "The most powerful and effective way for children to begin learning the complex process of learning about letters is by writing their own names." In addition to writing their own names I think exploring and playing with the letters in children's names is such a fun and meaningful way to introduce them to the alphabet.

My kids love their names and from young ages were most interested in the alphabet letters that they saw in their names. Since my kids are also very active, we have really enjoyed finding ways to channel their energy and find active ways to explore alphabet letters.

One favorite way that we like to play with alphabet letters is by going on hunts! Recently for Valentine's Day my seven-year-old decided to create an alphabet themed heart activity to help us learn the letters in our names.

To prep the activity we started off by cutting out a lot of hearts. Each child needed to cut out enough hearts so that they had one for each letter in their name. For example, Catie needed to cut out five hearts.

Once the hearts were cut out, we wrote a letter on each heart so that each child had a set of hearts with the letters from their name on them. For example, Catie had hearts with the letters c,a,t,i, and e on them.

Next we wrote each child's full name on a big piece of cardstock and then we hid all of the cut up alphabet hearts around our family room.

Each child then had to go and find all of the alphabet hearts that made up their name. Catie looked for the hearts that said c,a,t,i, or e on them.

Once each child had found all of their heart letters, they then tried to spell their name by putting the heart letters in order. Littler kids used the large cardstock name signs to help them while older kids put their names together without any help.

Once we were finished hunting and building the names, we then mixed up the letters and hid them again and started all over. My kids had fun playing this game over and over again until letters were lost or torn.

Although we created this heart version for Valentine's Day, this activity could easily be adapted for any theme or holiday.

discover·create·learn

Kristina Buskirk - Toddler Approved

Kristina is the founder of Toddler Approved. She is a mom of three (ages 7, 4 and 2), as well as a National Board certified teacher. Kristina taught for several years and then worked part-time as a curriculum specialist, new teacher coach, and crisis intervention trainer once she became a mom. She retired in the fall of 2011 and now loves being full-time mom and teacher to her kiddos. http://toddlerapproved.com/

DIY Bird's Nest Craft and Science

Fine Motor, Sensory, Science

Toddler

Pre-school

Kinder-garten

You will need:

White glue
Lots of string cut up into 5-6 inch lengths
Shredded paper
Spanish moss, or other decorative moss
Decorative grasses
Decorative feathers
A balloon and a small bowl
A BBQ skewer or sharp pencil to pop the balloon

How to:

Wouldn't you LOVE your child to make this stunningly realistic homemade bird's nest to hold their beautifully dyed Easter eggs this year? Can you believe that my two-and-a-half-year-old son basically made this nest by himself with very little assistance from me?

Learning about birds and spring, while developing a little "scientist" is all a part of this crafty bird's nest adventure!

Before you begin, you need to decide if you want your child's nest to look realistic. If so, choose natural-coloured materials. For a totally different look, provide brightly coloured string, shredded paper, and feathers!

Step 1. Blow up a small balloon so it fits nicely into a bowl the size of the nest that you want to make. In a large container, mix white glue with a little water to thin it out.

While you are getting started, this is a great time to discuss why birds make nests! What does your child think?

Step 2. Show your child how to dip the string into the glue and then squeeze it or run it between fingers to get the extra glue off. Then have your child place the string onto the balloon wherever they like. You may have to help with the first few pieces to get them started and feeling confident about the process. (It's okay to have too much glue - it just takes longer to dry!)

As your child works away, you can talk about how birds use all of these materials, plus sticks and twigs, to make their nests!

Step 3. Encourage your child to keep adding string and then eventually other materials until the balloon is covered.

While your child is building, ask them what they think birds use to keep the nest together instead of glue. (Answer: Mud! and lots of it!)

Step 4. Let the nest dry on the balloon for at least four hours. It's really hard for little ones to wait this long. I had to put our nest "out of sight" for a bit!

Step 5. The really fun part is last. Hand your child a BBQ skewer to pop the balloon!

We used our beautiful nest as a centrepiece for our Easter brunch - filled with brightly coloured eggs of course!

Sue Lively - One Time Through

Sue is a behaviour therapist, turned elementary school teacher, turned stay-at-home mom. On One Time Through, she shares her adventures of creating, observing, and celebrating life and parenthood with her favourite little guy, her preschool-aged son "Onetime!" http://onetimethrough.com/

ONE Time Through

Easy Easter Egg Garland

Fine Motor, Color Learning, Math, Counting

Toddler

Pre-school

Kinder-garten

You will need:

Embroidery floss
Plastic easter eggs

How to:

My kids and I love a good project. This little Easter Egg Garland was a really fun one to create with my two-year-old son, and gave him lots of great fine motor skill practice. Stringing objects is part of his upcoming skills check with our pediatrician's ages and stages questionnaire, so we've been working on it together. I thought making an egg garland would be great practice and give us a festive decoration for our mantle at the same time. He is so proud of his creation, as you can see. His two-year-old attention span couldn't handle making the whole thing in one day, so we worked on it bit by bit over several days.

The Bear chose green embroidery floss to make his garland, and we measured the length of the mantle to make sure it would be the right size. This boy LOVES to measure. I cut the thread and tied a slip knot in one end, creating a loop for easy hanging and stopping eggs from falling off the end. He picked out the colors and order and we practiced identifying colors as we went along. Sometimes he would poke the string through and I would pull it, sometimes the other way around. His favorite was reaching in to the egg to grab the string as I poked it through the hole. The eggs that are hinged together are the best for this particular project.

If I made this by myself, I would probably thread a needle and use it to expedite the process, but that wouldn't be safe with a toddler. We went along slowly and methodically, and he really loved it. We poked the thread through the hole in one end with the egg open, then out the hole at the other end. The Bear loved lifting the string and letting the egg fall down to the end. We counted as we went. Every time we started again we would measure and estimate how many more eggs we needed to finish. If you want to include pattern practice and recognition, you could easily add it to this project. It never ceases to amaze me how many skills can be practiced in a single, simple activity if I'm paying attention. This one project let us practice colors, numbers, counting, stringing objects, estimating, and measuring.

Becca Eby - Bare Feet on the Dashboard

Becca is a follower of Jesus, wife, and mother of two precious wee ones. She loves all things crafty and adventurous, and blogs about her frugal family, living debt free, home preschool, travel, homemaking, and parenting at Bare Feet on the Dashboard. http://www.barefeetonthedashboard.com/

Tie Dye Easter Eggs

Easter, Crafts

Toddler

Pre-school

Kinder-garten

You will need:

Markers
Baby wipes
Rubber bands
Eggs
Scissors

How to:

I love dying Easter eggs but I have to admit I would rather dye them by myself because I don't think little hands and big cups of dye go well together. Not wanting to leave my young kids out of the fun, I came up with an easy Easter egg coloring method. My toddler son (who was age one at the time) was even able to participate and I was able to enjoy the time together (instead of micromanaging any movement around cups of dye). Although I designed this activity for young kids, it's a pretty cool new way to decorate Easter eggs for any age...I loved it! The eggs turn out beautiful and bright, and unwrapping each one is a like a fun surprise to see how it turned out.

I poked a hole at the top and bottom of the eggs and blew the yoke out so the eggs would stay good until Easter. Also, I didn't want the marker to seep into the egg, making it inedible (no wasting food around here!) You don't have to blow the inside of your eggs out of the shell, but I would suggest not eating them because this activity uses markers and baby wipes. To blow the eggs out use a needle to poke a small hole at the top and bottom of your uncooked egg, stick a toothpick in the hole and stir to break up the yoke, and then at the top of the egg

blow the yoke into a bowl. It is surprisingly easy. If the yoke isn't coming out make the holes in your egg larger.

Directions:
Step 1. Cut baby wipes in half with scissors.

Step 2. Let kids draw on the baby wipes with markers. I used the fat Crayola markers. The more color on the wipes the better.

Tip: We made patterns on our wipes but the colors mix together as they transfer over. Our large designs with lots of colors turned out as our favorites.

Step 3. Wrap a baby wipe around each egg and gently secure it with a rubber band. Let the baby wipes dry. We set ours out overnight.

Once the eggs are dry unwrap the baby wipe and enjoy!

Katie Pinch - A Little Pinch of Perfect

Hi my name is Katie and I'm a busy mommy who can be found covered in paint or running wild in the backyard all to entertain my son and daughter. After studying Recreation Therapy and learning how to develop activities that facilitate learning through play, I became a stay-at-home mom and blogger so I could share all the fun activities we do with other parents looking for inspiration. http://www.alittlepinchofperfect.com/

Egg Lantern

Fine Motor, Sensory, Color Learning

Pre-school

Kinder-garten

You will need:

Balloon
Color tissue paper
Glue
Water
Battery operated tealight candle

How to:

The egg lantern is a simple yet interesting activity to do with kids. Every time I work on this project, my kids love the output. Since all the required materials are common household items, this project can be done with little or no preparation. Now let's see how to do an Egg Lantern.

Blow up the balloon and tie a knot. Mix glue with water in the ratio of 1:1. Encourage the kids to tear the tissue paper into pieces. Tearing paper provides an opportunity to work on their fine motor skills.

Dip the tissue paper in water. Place the tissue paper over the balloon to cover it leaving a small portion near the knot. There is no need to use glue mixture at this stage. At the end of the process, the balloon has to come out. Not using the glue for the first layer will ensure that the balloon comes out easily from the tissue paper.

Once the balloon is completely covered with tissue paper, for the second layer, use glue mixture to paste the tissue paper over the balloon. Three layers of tissue paper usually creates a beautiful lantern. Make sure that the balloon is not visible anywhere

except near the knot.

Let the tissue paper completely dry. Usually it takes three hours to dry. The drying time will vary depending on the weather conditions and the amount of glue used.

Once the balloon is completely dried, cut the balloon near the knot and carefully remove the balloon. As only water is used for the first layer, the balloon comes out easily. It looks like an inverted egg at this stage.

Cover the hole in the egg with tissue paper. Make a small hole at the opposite side just enough to fit the tea light candle.

Place the tea light candle at the table and cover it with the tissue paper egg.

Enjoy the beautifully lit egg lantern!

Dhiyana - Edutainment At Home

Dhiyana is a Software Engineer, mom to two daughters and wife of an amazing man. She is the creator behind www.sparklingbuds.blogspot.com that focuses on art, craft and playful learning ideas for kids. She documents her activity ideas in her mother tongue Tamil at www.dheekshu.blogspot.com

Contact Paper Flowers

Sensory

Toddler

Pre-school

Kinder-garten

You will need:

Clear contact paper
Tissue paper in many colors
Pipe cleaners
Large colorful buttons
Hot glue/hot glue gun
Scissors

How to:

Instead of a bouquet of real flowers to give to Mom for Mother's Day, try making some of these crafty flowers that she'll get to keep for year and years!

These are simple enough for toddlers to take part in making, as well as older kids!

Kids can start by cutting up different colors of tissue paper, which sneaks in some scissors practice.

If kids don't know how to use scissors yet (this would be a great way to introduce them!) they can tear up the tissue paper with their hands. It's still great fine motor practice for them!

Any color of tissue paper works well for this craft. But we had lots of bright colors as well as tissue paper with dots and stars on it, too. Those were my kids' favorites.

Once tissue paper is cut into small pieces (about an inch in size), lay out a piece of contact paper, sticky side up on the table.

Tape the contact paper down to stop it from curling under. Scotch tape in the corners or painter's tape all around it works well!

The kids can then stick their cut up pieces of tissue paper that they cut onto the contact paper to make a tissue paper collage.

Then flatten it out as much as possible by pressing down all the tissue paper. Then cover it with another piece of contact paper to sandwich the tissue paper in between.

Then older kids can get more cutting practice, or this would be better for adults to do. Cut lots of flower shapes out of the tissue paper collage! Freehand it or draw them on first.

Kids can choose the perfect button and pipe cleaner for each flower. Using the hot glue gun, secure the button in the center of the flower. Try letting the kids have a try at the hot glue gun too!

Hot glue the pipe cleaner to the back of the flower too to be the stem.

Repeat as many times as you have flowers! Tie them all up in a ribbon for a pretty bouquet for Mom or Grandma for Mother's Day.

Jamie Reimer - hands on : as we grow

Jamie learned to be a hands on mom by creating activities, crafts and art projects for her three boys to do. As a former marketing manager, Jamie needs the creative outlet to get through the early years of parenting with a smile!
http://handsonaswegrow.com/

Rainbow Footprint Butterfly

Sensory, Color Learning

Baby

Toddler

Pre-school

Kinder-garten

You will need:

Rainbow coloured poster paint
Thick paper, card or a mini canvas
Black marker pen

How to:

A footprint butterfly would make a perfect keepsake for Mother's Day. Crafts that capture a child's tiny prints are extra special as children really don't stay small for long. This butterfly would look great framed or painted onto a mini canvas and the rainbow colours would brighten up any room. Alternatively, it would be a great idea for a Mother's Day card or greeting card.

How to make a Rainbow Footprint Butterfly
Step 1. Squirt some rainbow-coloured poster paint onto a plate.

Step 2. Paint your child's feet using the rainbow coloured paints. Start at the toes and paint a stripe across their feet in each of your rainbow colours. You will have to work quite quickly as you don't want the paint to start drying.

Step 3. Press your child's feet onto a piece of paper (or mini canvas) to create a butterfly shape. The outer edge of each foot needs to be in the middle of the butterfly design. Keep the two prints quite close together but leave enough room to draw on your butterfly's body.

Step 4. Once the paint is completely dry, get a black marker pen and draw your butterfly's body between the two wings.

TIPS: Older children will be happy to sit still (or do the painting themselves if they are extra flexible), but if you are trying to paint a baby's feet I would have somebody on standby to help. For babies or small children the easiest way I have found to take the prints is to press the paper onto their feet whilst they are sitting down, (but they will probably still end up covered in paint!).

Louise McMullen - Messy Little Monster

Louise is mum to two gorgeous children, a teacher and writer of 'Messy Little Monster.' She loves anything arty and has a fun, creative approach to playing and learning. Messy Little Monster is a kid's activity blog full of art, craft and activity ideas to inspire you. http://messylittlemonster.com/

How to Make Paper Flowers

Fine Motor, Color Learning, Size Sorting

Pre-school

Kinder-garten

You will need:

Heavy weight white paper
Black tempera paint
Two flower or snowflake cookie cutters ~ different sizes
Watercolor paints
Scissors
Wooden skewers
Glue
Colorful buttons

How to:

Flowers just seem fitting for spring and Mother's Day, don't they? While the real deal are gorgeous, this paper version allows your kids to add their own personal touch. They can choose any color combination they want, and the best part...no watering necessary! Totally a win in my books. Read on for a super quick and easy tutorial for how to make paper flowers with your kids.

Your first step is to create the flower petals. You will need two different sizes of flower/snowflake cookie cutters (we used snowflakes), black paint, a tray and heavy white paper. Pour a small amount of black paint onto a paint tray/paper plate. Dip the cookie cutter into the paint and stamp onto the paper. Repeat until the entire paper resembles a giant coloring book dotted with beautiful flower outlines.

Have you tried stamping with cookie cutters before? Its one of our go-to preschool activities because it's simple to set up, easy and adaptable to most any holiday.

Once the flower outlines are dry, you are ready to add a splash of color with watercolor paints. This is your moment to get creative, there is no right or wrong color combo. Honestly, I love the look of multiple colors in each flower, so the more color the better! Roll your sleeves up and get creative. Since they will be cut out, no need to worry about painting outside the lines.

Once the petals are completely dry, you will need to cut each one out. This is the perfect time to work on scissor skills. We chose to keep the black outlines when we were cutting; I think it adds a little extra character. I also love the ones where the cookie cutter "jumped" a little and there is a double impression.

Now you're ready to put your flowers together. For each one, you will need to make 2 large and two small petals, a wooden skewer and a large brightly colored button. Glue and sandwich the skewer between the two large petals. Next glue the two smaller petals onto the center of the large one. Finally, top everything off with a large colorful button. Simply repeat until you have all the flowers you need for your bouquet.

Paper flowers are a great alternative to real ones; they're quick and easy to make, plus you can customize them with any colors or patterns you want! Love it! Perfect for Mother's Day or to give as a gift to someone special.

Tammy - Housing A Forest

Hello. I'm Tammy. The writer, creator and girl behind the camera of Housing A Forest, a blog that focuses on kids activities. I love messy projects, hands on learning and discovering the world from a kid's point of view. Being a busy mom of 3 school-aged kids; running an in-home daycare and teaching high school art keeps me on my toes. In my spare time, I love dumpster diving, garage sales and yummy coffee. http://www.housingaforest.com/

DIY Fingerprint Tie

Fine Motor, Sensory, Play Recipes, Color Learning, Math, Counting, Shapes

- Baby
- Toddler
- Pre-school
- Kinder-garten

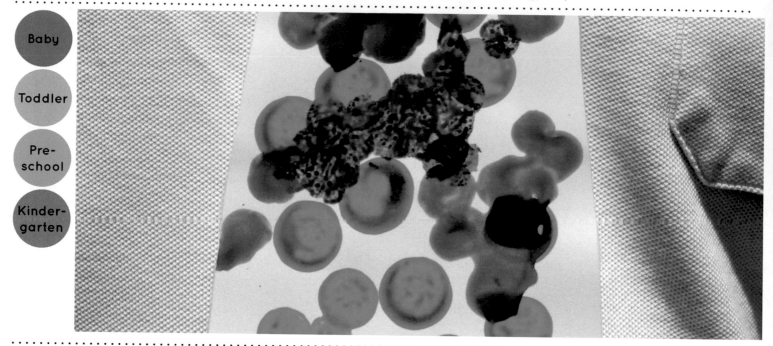

You will need:

Two sheets card stock paper (white)
Washable paint (This is only if you want to use paint to make real "fingerprints". If not, you could use markers to make dots, or use those dotters that they sell at the store to make dots)
Marker (to write on the back)
Picture of your child (or your child with his/her dad)
Glue (to glue the two ties together)
Yarn (to hold it onto dad's neck)
Non-heat laminating sheets (You can buy these at Walmart. I used the AVERY brand)

How to:

For Father's Day, our three year old son made this adorable craft and my husband loves it!! It is a two-sided DIY fingerprint tie craft for Father's Day - and Dad can wear it!

Step 1. Put the two sheets of cardstock out – one on top of the other.

Step 2. Cut out a tie shape (you will end up with two ties.)

Step 3. On the one tie, you will use the marker to write "I LOVE YOU, DAD" and glue the picture onto the bottom.

Step 4. On the second tie, you will make fingerprints with the different colors of (washable) paint.
IMPORTANT: You will be having both decorated ties facing out, so be sure that they line up properly!!

Step 5. After they dry, glue them together, with the decorated side facing out.
After that dries, cover it with the laminate paper.

Step 6. Cut holes (or use a hole-punch) into the top corners and thread a piece of yarn through it, to tie it onto Dad's neck.

Give it to Dad and watch him SMILE!

Becky Mansfield - Your Modern Family

Becky Mansfield runs yourmodernfamily.com where she posts parenting tips to raise kids in the modern world. She is the author of Potty Train in a Weekend, You Can be a Stay at Home Mom on One Income and Freed From Clutter, as well as the book Blogging on the Side. http://www.yourmodernfamily.com/

Foam Tie Key Ring

Crafts, Father's Day

Toddler

Pre-school

Kinder-garten

You will need:

Key rings - the bigger the key ring, the bigger you can make the tie
Craft foam
Glue
Additional craft foam pieces/shapes as decorations
Other decorative items you want to add
Puffy paint or glitter glue if you want to use that to decorate the ties

How to:

Father's Day is around the corner! Here is a quick and easy but sweet gift for Dad or Grandad!

Cut a double tie shape out of the craft foam by folding the piece of craft foam double, then cutting it so that the two pieces are exactly the same. The size will depend on your key ring size; it should fit inside the ring when you fold the two parts together.

Place the key ring on the fold and close it so that the two pieces fit onto each other. Use glue to stick the two pieces together if you don't use the sticky craft foam type.

Now decorate as you wish.

For the green tie, I've used craft foam dots.
The silver tie was already glittery, but one can add glitter to a plain craft foam piece too.

The blue tie had stripes added with puffy paint.

The possibilities are endless! The result is so cute, I'm sure any dad will love it!

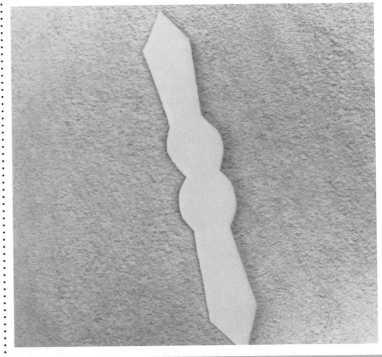

Nadia - Teach me Mommy

Nadia is a teacher turned mommy to two blessings. She blogs over at Teach me Mommy about easy and playful activities with the aim to teach. http://teach-me-mommy.com

Upcycled Nuts and Bolts Heart Craft

Toddler

Pre-school

Kinder-garten

You will need:

Canvas
Nuts and bolts, nails, washers, screws, etc.
Wooden letters (optional) that spell the word that you choose
Non-toxic heavy duty glue (Lots of glue - not school glue)
Spray paint
A covered, well-ventilated work space

How to:

You can put all of those random nuts and bolts that you have in your garage to good use with this upcycled nuts and bolts heart craft.

My husband is a pack rat and I am a minimalist, so this upcycled nuts and bolts heart is a fabulous way to combine both of our personalities to make one great gift. I don't know if your husband is like mine but for some reason every nut, bolt, nail or random spare part must be saved. I decided to put these random items to good use by adding some love and a little craftiness. I thought that it was especially clever to use my husband's random items to make a gift for him. While my son was making this craft we talked about what he likes about his dad. A homemade gift is so much better when love and gratitude is highlighted.

How to make an upcycled nuts and bolts heart:

• First, outline the shape that you want to make with pencil and apply the glue to outline the shape.

• Then glue the nuts, screws, bolts and washers inside the shape.
• After the upcycled items are glued onto the surface in the shape that you made, glue on the letters to make the word that you chose.
• Allow the upcycled nuts and bolts craft plenty of time to dry. Once it has dried, take the spray paint and liberally cover with the spray paint. Be sure to do this step in a well-ventilated area.
• Allow the upcycled nuts and bolts heart plenty of time to dry.

Now you have a beautiful gift for someone your child loves. My son's upcycled nuts and bolts heart proudly hangs in his dad's office so that my husband can be reminded every day that he is appreciated and loved. We made this craft for Father's Day but it could be used for so many occasions. Your child could make this as a special Valentine for someone they love. It could be a birthday present or just a sweet craft to make for a grandparent.

Shelah - Mosswood Connections

Shelah Moss is an autism consultant, tutor and mother. Her goal in life is to continue to learn and teach while having fun. http://mosswoodconnections.com/

Salt Dough Baseballs

Fine Motor, Sensory, Play Recipes

Pre-school

Kinder-garten

You will need:

1 cup flour
1 cup salt
1/2 cup water
Circle cookie cutter or drinking glass
Drinking straw
Toothpicks
Foil-lined baking sheet
Red and white acrylic paint
Yarn or string

How to:

Salt dough baseballs are a fun gift that kids can make for their baseball-loving dads. Salt dough is fun to work with and very easy to make. Your little ones can easily make this Father's Day keepsake.

To make the salt dough, mix together 1 cup flour and 1 cup salt. After the dry ingredients are mixed together, add ½ cup water. Mix until combined. Your mixture should have a play dough consistency. If it's too dry, add more water a teaspoon at a time. If it's too wet, add more flour a teaspoon at a time. Knead the dough until it is soft and firm.

Take some time to play with the dough. It's very similar to play dough, only grittier because of all the salt. Playing with the dough for awhile will not affect the project. After you're done kneading and playing with the dough, it's time to get to work making your baseballs. Roll out the dough to about a quarter-inch thick. Use a circle cookie cutter or a drinking glass to make your baseball shape.

Use your drinking straw to make your hole in the top of each baseball. You'll be adding string through the hole once the baseballs are dry and painted. Dad will be able to hang it up at work or near his favorite sports-watching chair.

Use toothpicks to add the stitching details on the baseballs. Try not to poke all the way through your baseballs; the stitching should be on the surface.

Once you're done, place your baseballs on a foil-lined baking sheet. Place them in a 250 degree F oven for a couple of hours or until they are dry and hard. Once dry, use your acrylic paint to paint your baseballs. When the paint is dry, add your string through the hole. Let your baseballs rest for a couple of days before hanging just to ensure that they are dry all the way through.

Dad will love receiving this fun baseball gift from the kids!

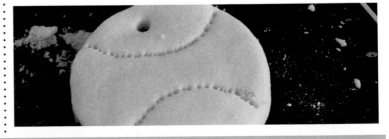

Terri Thompson - Creative Family Fun

You can often find Terri crafting at the kitchen table with her two girls, puttering in the garden, or cooking up a masterpiece. She is the creator of Creative Family Fun (http://creativefamilyfun.net), where you will find hundreds of activities to help you spend some meaningful time with your kids.

Popsicle Stick American Flag Craft

Toddler

Pre-school

Kinder-garten

You will need:

13 wooden craft sticks
Paint (red, white and blue)
Paint brush
Razor blade and cutting board
Sandpaper
String
Tacky glue

How to:

This American Flag craft is simple to make for children of all ages. Please note that wooden craft sticks are difficult to cut in half without proper tools and should be handled in advance by the parent.

Step 1. Prep four craft sticks for the blue field by carefully cutting sticks in half with your razor blade. You can also get a saw, but that seems like overkill.
Step 2. Use sandpaper to smooth the cut edges of the sticks. Don't have sandpaper? Use an emery board!
Step 3. Paint the half sticks blue. Then paint five sticks red and four sticks white. You can also leave four sticks unpainted for a more rustic look. Allow sticks to dry.
Step 4. Place the remaining two unpainted sticks on your work surface vertically–these are the support frame. Dot with glue. Place red and white sticks horizontally, starting with red. Leave room at the top for the string.
Step 5. Glue blue half sticks to the upper left corner. Allow to dry.

Step 6. Paint polka dot "stars" on the blue field. To make the dots, dip the opposite end of a paint brush in paint and gently tap onto the sticks. Let your child practice first on an extra stick to see how big the dots are–more paint, bigger dot! Allow to dry.
Step 7. Tie string around upper vertical craft stick to make a hanger. I wrapped the string around a couple times, tied, then dabbed with glue to hold it securely in place.

Denise Bertacchi - stlMotherhood

Denise is a Midwestern mom of two boys who loves writing, crafting and playing video games. She's been a freelance newspaper reporter, a online columnist and a blogger. http://stlMotherhood.com/

President Stick Puppets

Pre-school

Kinder-garten

You will need:

Coins (1 per puppet)
Construction paper
Glue
Popsicle sticks (1 per puppet)
Scissors

Optional:
Stickers
Markers
Magazines

How to:

These president stick puppets are a fantastic way of opening the door for a discussion on American history as well as an easy small world play toy that your preschooler can make for themselves. Just follow these simple steps:

Step 1. Gather your supplies. It is always easier to complete a project when you start off with everything you need already on hand.
Step 2. Have your child use scissors to cut out a simple shirt shape from the construction paper. Depending on their age, you may just want to cut this out for them, or draw a picture of a shirt that they can cut out. Older children should be able to do this step on their own.
Step 3. Glue the construction paper shirt to the popsicle stick, leaving about a half inch at the top for the puppet's head to be attached.

Step 4. Glue the coin to the top of popsicle stick head side up. This is your puppet's head.
If you want to keep things easy, you can let the glue dry and be done. It is already a fun and functional president stick puppet.

Optional Idea 1:
Decorate the puppet's shirt with stickers, markers, etc.

Optional Idea 2:
Cut another piece of construction paper out in the shape of a hat. Make a tricorne for George Washington, a top hat for Abraham Lincoln.

Alternative Idea:
Instead of using construction paper, cut out pictures of shirts and hats from magazines.
A few quick facts to keep in mind when playing with these president stick puppets:
- George Washington was our 1st president. He served from 1789-1797.
- Thomas Jefferson was our 3rd president. He served from 1801-1809.
- Abraham Lincoln was our 16th president. He served from 1861-1865.
- Franklin Roosevelt was our 32nd president. He served from 1933-1945.

Caitlyn "Suzy" Stock - Suzy Homeschooler

Caitlyn is a geeky mom of two who writes about homeschooling ideas, activities, and lesson plans.
http://suzyhomeschooler.com/

Fourth of July Firework Art

Fine Motor, Sensory

Toddler

Pre-school

You will need:

Finger paints - red, yellow, green, blue, other
Paper for painting
1 wire scrub brush (circular)
12 pipe cleaners (for two pipe cleaner paint brushes)
5-10 large pompoms
Circular kitchen bottlebrush

How to:

Do you need several creative and fast art ideas for Fourth of July? Let me share with you four festive firework art ideas that simply use items found around the house. Grab the finger paints, your happy children, and several items for painting fireworks. Here are four examples of items that can be used to paint fireworks: wire scrub brush (circular), several pipe cleaners, large pompoms, and a circular kitchen bottlebrush. These four items will design some fantastic firework art.

First of all, set up a workspace for your child's messy play. Maybe a special kid art table, the kitchen table with a disposable plastic tablecloth, or an art tray that is used only for painting. The point it to create a space for your child that is a safe spot for making a fun mess. Place paper down on the surface of the workspace and prepare the finger paints in a bowl. Place a large dollop of paint into a bowl. You can have the paint be one color or a mix of several colors slightly swirled together. Take note to not mix the paints completely together. You want to have several colors that are slightly mixed but distinctly their own color still.

Now let's get started with painting our amazing fireworks! Give your child one of the art mediums to use - the wire scrub brush, large pompoms, or circular kitchen bottlebrush. Explain to them that they can dip the art medium (wire scrub brush, pompoms, bottlebrush) into the colors and use it to paint with. Watch your child's expression as they see the unique firework shapes that appear on their art paper.

The pipe cleaner fireworks take a little more effort to prepare. If you have a preschool -aged child, let them help you make the pipe cleaner paintbrush. Gather six pipe cleaners and twirl them together on one end. Twirl them half way down and then with the remaining half bend the pipe cleaners out to create a fan shaped look. Now the pipe cleaner paintbrush is ready to be used. Dip it into a larger bowl of finger paints and have fun! Talk with your child about how each firework shape is distinctly different and ask them which one they like the best. Enjoy!

Vanessa - Mama's Happy Hive

Vanessa enjoys discovering and learning the beauty of hands-on Montessori education with her toddler. She finds this learning journey to be one of the most delightful journeys she has ever taken and looks forward to the years of continued discovery with her little one as he grows up. http://www.mamashappyhive.com/

Permanent Marker Fireworks T-Shirt

Fine Motor, Color Learning, Science, Science Experiments

Kinder-garten

You will need:

T-shirt
Permanent (sharpie) markers
Rubbing alcohol
Medicine dropper
Cardboard

How to:

You'll see fireworks with this fun, fine motor activity that also creates a celebratory Fourth of July T-shirt!

Safety first! Make sure the children are old enough to know not to drink the rubbing alcohol and do this activity in a well-ventilated area.

Step 1. Place cardboard in between the front and back layers of the t-shirt. Make dots with your sharpie marker in a circle shape.

Step 2. Use the dropper to drop rubbing alcohol into the center of the design. The marker will spread. (TRY-IT: What happens if you use water, instead?)

Step 3. Experiment with concentric circles of dots, dashes, spirals...anything in a circular shape should work. The metallic Sharpie permanent markers didn't run with alcohol, so we used those to write words or numbers.

Step 4. After the shirt is completely dry (the alcohol is flammable), run the shirt through the dryer or iron on the reverse side before washing.

Wear with patriotic pride!

Science Connection: Why do the Sharpie designs run and blend in rubbing alcohol but not in water?

Candace Lindemann - Naturally Educational

Candace Lindemann is a nationally recognized and quoted educational expert and published children's writer. She blogs about learning projects and ideas in education at Naturally Educational and creates custom curricula, textbook materials and content for educational publishing, entertainment, technology and toy companies.
http://NaturallyEducational.com/

Halloween Memory Game for Kids

DIY Toys

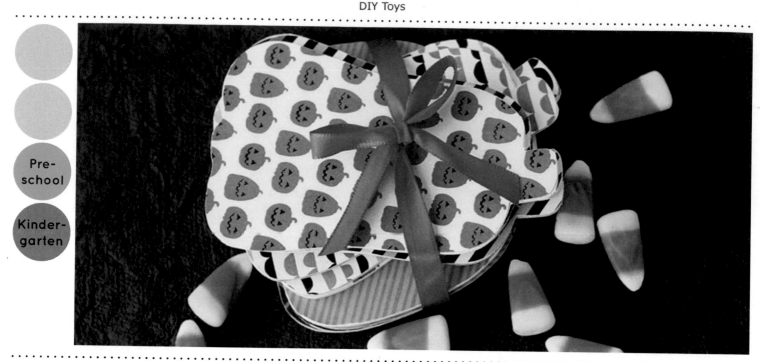

Pre-school

Kinder-garten

You will need:

Halloween scrapbook paper
Wooden pumpkin shapes (I purchased from Hobby Lobby)
Double-sided tape
Scissors or X-ACTO knife with cutting mat

How to:

Halloween is just around the corner! My boys are excited, as they love the costumes, candy, and spooky decorations. My youngest son recently asked, "Do babies like Halloween?" He was thinking about his cousin who is just a little over one and added, "She can't eat candy and she might get scared." We decided to send her a book and a homemade Halloween Memory Game to wish her a very Happy Halloween!

I have a passion for super easy, low-cost crafts for kids. This memory game is no exception. I purchased all of the supplies on clearance and kept assembly very simple.

Step 1. Trace the pumpkin shapes onto the white side of the scrapbook paper, as pictured below.

Step 2. Cut out the shapes with scissors or an X-ACTO knife. Attach the scrapbook paper to the wooden shapes using double-sided tape. If desired, seal the game pieces with Mod Podge.

Step 3. Flip the cards wood-side up, and play! The person who collects the most pairs, wins. Babies will enjoy exploring the vibrant colors and patterns on each of the cards. Challenge

preschoolers to create repeating patterns with the shapes. There are so many fun ways to play and learn!

Melissa Lennig - Fireflies and Mud Pies

Fireflies + Mud Pies
Simple crafts and play for kids!

Melissa Lennig is the voice behind Fireflies and Mud Pies, a children's activity blog that is packed with inexpensive activities and crafts to encourage families to play, create, and celebrate childhood. Social-emotional growth, nature crafts, outdoor play, and "from scratch" cooking are just a few of our passions. Melissa shares creative, low-cost ideas for learning, connecting, and playing at home. http://www.firefliesandmudpies.com/

Counting & Number Recognition

Fine Motor, Color Learning, Math, Counting

Toddler

Pre-school

You will need:

Construction paper
Markers
M&M's, Reese's Pieces or other candy
Laminator

How to:

Most kids love candy, especially mine. So when I can use candy to encourage my kids to do educational activities, it's always a win for me. This simple activity is really quick and easy to put together and gives toddlers and preschoolers the opportunity to practice pre-math skills like counting and number recognition. It's also an activity that's easily modified to fit the different seasons and holidays- or done any time of the year depending on how you choose to create it.

For a Halloween version of the activity, draw pumpkins on a sheet of construction paper. Cut out the pumpkins. If your child is practicing scissor skills, have them cut out the pumpkins themselves. Then write the numbers 1-10 on the pumpkins, one number for each pumpkin. If you want to give your kids a little extra help, you can also add dots that correspond to the written number so they can count them if they get stuck. If you have a laminator, you can laminate the pumpkins to make them a little sturdier.

To complete the activity, give your child a pile of M&M's or Reese's pieces and encourage them to match each number with the correct number of candy pieces. You can also suggest they sort the candy by color, or they might even do it naturally. As you play, you can also demonstrate pattern making with the candy.

At Christmas, make the shapes Christmas trees or use hearts for Valentine's Day. All of these holidays usually involve candy anyway, so you can use the extra you have on hand to let the kids enjoy their sweets while learning at the same time.

For an everyday version of this activity, use a bowl or something circular shaped to cut circles out of construction paper. This version of the activity is also great for kids to practice sorting and learning colors.

Cut out the circles (red, blue, green, orange, yellow, and brown). Write the numbers 1-10 with one number on each circle and complete the activity by asking your child to match the correct number of candy pieces with the number on the circle. They can also separate their candy by color. Then enjoy a candy treat when they're finished.

Amy Pessolano - Umbrella Tree Cafe

Amy Pessolano is a freelance writer and mom to two active, energetic boys. She's on a mission to raise creative, curious, lifelong learners. You can find her ideas for simple educational activities and art projects, plus more inspiration on her blog Umbrella Tree Cafe. http://amypessolano.com/

Easy Grocery Bag Ghosts

Gross Motor, DIY Toys, Imagination Play

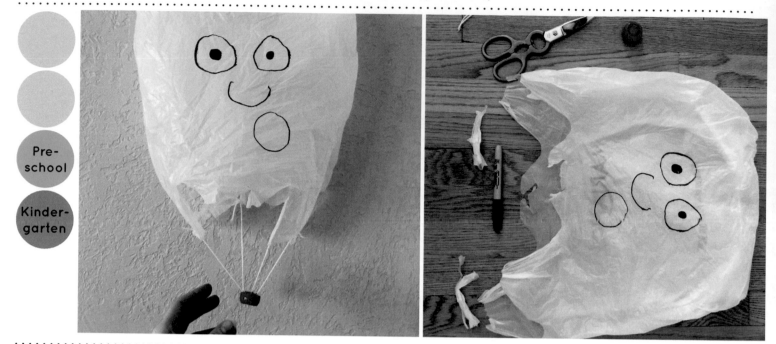

Pre-school

Kinder-garten

You will need:

Plastic grocery bag
String
Small item for weight, such as a LEGO man, felt finger puppet, coin, etc.
Scissors
Permanent marker

How to:

Using the permanent marker, you or your child can draw a ghost face on the bag. Use your scissors to snip off the handles of the bag, about an inch above where they are joined. Snip 4 small holes in the bag, 1 per handle section, about a half inch from where you just cut the handles.

Cut two lengths of string (ours were about a foot long each but you can experiment with different lengths and different weighted items). Feed the string through the spokes of the pouch cap or tie it to your weight in the center of the strings. Tie one end of the strings through each of the small holes you snipped in the handles. Puff the bag out a little, give it a toss and watch it float down! Spooooooky! Repeat the steps to make lots of ghosts!

Other Ways to Use the Ghosts
You can also use the ghosts without the string and weight! We taped them to our windows for Halloween decorations.

You could also use them to make a Halloween obstacle course! Tape a few ghosts to the underside of your dining room table.

Be sure to add something past the edge of the table as a reminder not to stand up too early.

We put a spooky spider a foot past the table and kept reminding each other we had to crawl through the ghosts and past the spiders before we could stand up. Add a few other spooky obstacles other places around the house, like a few pumpkins to run around, and an easy costume to put on as part of the obstacle course. Be sure to demonstrate all the obstacles yourself...what a fun way to get down and play with the kids!

Laura Marschel - Lalymom

Laura is a Chicagoland stay-at-home mom to two sweet redheads who fuel all the fun and creativity you find at Lalymom. You'll see fine motor skills activities, DIY toys, fun printables and more! http://www.lalymom.com/

Mason Jar Jack-O-Lantern Craft

Fine Motor

Pre-school

Kinder-garten

You will need:

Mason jar
Orange tissue paper squares
Black construction paper
Mod Podge or watered down glue
Paint brush
Scissors
Battery-powered LED light

How to:

Our family enjoys carving pumpkins every Halloween to decorate our front porch. The only problem with our Halloween jack-o-lanterns is that they quickly begin to rot! This means we have to carve them just a day or two before Halloween to ensure they last through the holiday.

Wanting a jack-o-lantern that we would be able to display throughout the month of October, I came up with an idea to create jack-o-lanterns using Mason jars. The best thing about our mason jar jack-o-lanterns is they can adorn our living room all October long and I never have to worry about them rotting. Plus, they look amazing lit up at night. And best of all, my kids feel so proud to see their artwork displayed for all to see.

Involving kids in making this Mason jar jack-o-lantern craft helps them develop skills that include:

- Creativity: children design faces for their jack-o-lanterns
- Fine motor skills: children strengthen their finger muscles as they work with a paint brush
- Understanding of spatial relationships: children consider where each element of their jack-o-lantern's face goes in relation to the other elements

To make your Mason jar jack-o-lantern craft, follow these steps:

Step 1. Use a paint brush to apply Mod Podge or watered down glue to the outside of your Mason jar.

Step 2. Cover your Mason jar with orange tissue paper squares.

Step 3. Add another layer of mod podge or watered down glue over the tissue paper to ensure it all lays flat. You may want to repeat steps 2 and 3 until you have several layers of tissue paper covering your entire mason jar.

Step 4. Once your Mason jar is covered in orange tissue paper, cut shapes from your black construction paper in order to make your jack-o-lantern's eyes, nose, mouth, etc.

Step 5. Use Mod Podge or watered down glue to stick the construction paper shapes on your Mason jar in the form of a face.

Step 6. Once your Mason jar has finished drying, place a small, battery-powered LED light inside your jack-o-lantern.

Step 7. In a dark room, switch on your jack-o-lantern's LED light. Then enjoy your beautiful Halloween creation!

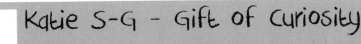

Katie S-G - Gift of Curiosity

Gift of CURIOSITY
Sparking children's creativity and learning

Katie is the creative force behind Gift of Curiosity, a resource site for parents, teachers, and caregivers who want to engage children in hands-on, developmentally appropriate educational activities. Katie has a master's degree in education and a Ph.D. in child development. She is also the mom of two curious kids, who provide inspiration for most of the ideas she shares. http://www.giftofcuriosity.com/

Halloween Sensory Bin

Fine Motor, Sensory, Imagination Play, Color Learning, Math, Counting

Pre-school

Kinder-garten

You will need:

Container (we use an under-bed storage box)
Black water beads
A range of kitchen utensils and containers
Insects
Reptiles

How to:

Sensory bins are great for stimulating the senses through hands-on learning. We really like how you can theme your bins to topics and your child's interests.
Sensory Bins are a fun, interesting way to introduce new themes. This is the Halloween Sensory Bin we created.

The day before we set about preparing the water beads. It took 4 packets of 10g to get a good coverage in this large under-the-bed storage box. We sprinkled the tiny beads into water and covered the container.
They take around eight to twelve hours to fully expand, so I find leaving them overnight is perfect.

I then added different insects and lizards to the water bead base and had a variety of bowls, containers and kitchen utensils available for play. The water beads are great for scooping up, then filling and emptying containers. They feel silky smooth to touch.

If you submerge the expanded water beads into water they provide another fun sensory experience that is well worth

exploring too! We used the beads to hide the spiders and insects and we had fun trying to find them again. Water beads can be used more than once, just simply allow the water to drain and they will shrink back down to tiny little balls.

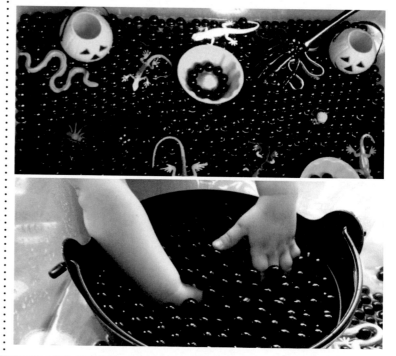

Amy Powell - Learning and Exploring Through Play

Amy is a stay-at-home mom with a background in education. She is passionate about children learning through their play and that is the driving force behind her blog. Learning and Exploring Through Play is full of inspiring arts, crafts and sensory play ideas for children. http://learningandexploringthroughplay.com/

Tissue Paper Pumpkin Craft

Fine Motor

Pre-school

Kinder-garten

You will need:

Styrofoam ball
Orange tissue paper (different shades)
Brown pipe cleaner
Green and black construction paper
Paint Brush
White craft glue
Water
Container with lid
Glue stick
Scissors

How to:

The holidays are one of our favorite times for creating fun and messy crafts. Creating fun pumpkin crafts for Halloween is always a must, but the messier they are the cuter they turn out! Let me warn you... this might get a bit messy!

Step 1. Gather your different shades of tissue paper and lay them flat on top of each other. Cut them into strips and then cut those strips into squares. You will end up with a large pile of orange shaded squares.

Step 2. Create your own Mod Podge with white craft glue and water. Pour 1/2 cup of white craft glue and 1/2 cup of water into a container with a lid. Shake for about a minute or until everything is combined. Just remember it's equal amounts of glue to water.

Step 3. To keep your Styrofoam ball from rolling around, push down on a flat surface to create a flat bottom. Now you are ready to begin adding your tissue paper.

Step 4. Dip your paint brush into your homemade Mod Podge and brush a small section at a time on your Styrofoam ball. After each brush add a piece of orange square tissue paper, until you have covered your entire ball. Don't be afraid to add too many layers or too much glue, just remember, this part can get sticky and messy. Help younger children glue on their tissue paper.

Step 5. Allow your pumpkin to dry overnight. You might need a few nights depending on how much glue was used.

Step 6. Once your pumpkin is fully dry go ahead and add a face using black construction paper. Cut out some triangles for eyes and a smile or scary teeth for the mouth. Glue on your pumpkin using glue sticks.

Step 7. Time to create a stem for your pumpkin using pipe cleaners. Have your child wrap the pipe cleaners around their fingers. Gently pull off and you will have a twisty stem perfect for your pumpkin. To attach your stem, just push it down in your Styrofoam pumpkin.

Step 8. Cut out a small leaf with construction paper and glue on your stem.

This is such a great fun craft for kids to do during Halloween, but it also provides a fun way for them to practice their fine motor skills and creativity!

Victoria Armijo - ABC Creative Learning

ABC creative LEARNING
where ideas bloom

Hi I'm Victoria! Wife and mommy of two amazing little girls! I blog over at ABC Creative Learning, where I share homeschooling ideas, kid crafts, recipes, and our love of theme parks! http://abccreativelearning.com/

Halloween Countdown

Sensory, Math, Counting

Toddler

Pre-school

Kinder-garten

Printable

You will need:

Countdown chart
Sheet of black or orange card stock or construction paper
Glue
White Cotton balls

How to:

Once the weather turns cooler, I will very frequently hear "How many more days until I can wear my costume?"

Can you relate?

It's hard for children to understand the passing of time, so a countdown activity helps them become aware of how many more days they will need to wait until the impending holiday. This countdown activity also offers your child a chance to practice their number recognition and math skills as they look forward to the coming of Halloween.

Print or copy the ghost template on white paper. Then have your child cut out the shape and glue it to a black or orange sheet of paper in order to make the chart sturdier since they will be attaching cotton balls to it throughout the month.

Children of all ages will enjoy the sensory aspect of this activity as they play with the cotton balls.

Each day in October, have your child search for the date on the ghost and glue a cotton ball over that number. For extra practice,

ask them to count how many cotton balls are on the chart each day and then find the next number.

Preschoolers are beginning to recognize some of their numbers, so daily counting practice can really reinforce their math skills. Younger children can use this as a number-matching activity. Write out the date or show them the date on a calendar and then have them search for the same number on the countdown chart.

If you have kids who are able to count to 31, ask them to do the countdown backwards (counting from 31 to 1 instead of counting forward).

For children who are proficient at counting, ask them to do some mental math by calculating how many days are left until Halloween using subtraction -- for example, on October 5th, they would need to mentally calculate $31 - 5 = 26$ days remaining until the holiday.

Number recognition, sensory fun and a holiday calendar all wrapped up in one!

Jacquie Fisher - Edventures with Kids

Jacquie is an educator, writer and Mom to 2 creative kids! She is the founder of Edventures with Kids where she shares ideas for kids activities, children's literature, family travel and fun ways to learn. When she's not writing, Jacquie enjoys outdoor activities, baking, reading children's literature and traveling with her family.
http://www.kcedventures.com/blog

3-D Thanksgiving Turkey Art

Fine Motor, Sensory

Pre-school

Kinder-garten

You will need:

A cardboard egg carton
Scissors
Tempera paint
A paintbrush
Cotton balls
Clear-drying school glue
Googly eyes
Cardstock paper

How to:

Thanksgiving with kids usually equals lots of turkey-themed arts and crafts! We have a lot of wild turkeys roaming through my neighborhood (seriously, I saw one walking into the drive-through door of the carwash – I guess he needed a bath).

Do you really want your preschooler making a realistic turkey? I can almost guarantee you that it won't be anything that you'll want to display at your holiday dinner. In real-life, they aren't the most majestic of birds. Instead, why not make a cuddly, cute-looking little Thanksgiving pal?

I was about to toss an egg carton when it occurred to me that I could reuse it to make a 3-D turkey craft. Let your child get in touch with texture, shape and form during this holiday-inspired art activity.

Here's What to Do:
Step 1. Cut the egg carton so that you have two compartments and a divider together. Each compartment will become an eye, and the divider will become the beak.

Step 2. Cut a larger section of at least four compartments to make the body.

Step 3. Pour paint into the remaining egg carton compartments. Use fall colors such as yellow, brown, orange and red.

Step 4. Mix the paint into custom turkey colors. Your child can use the extra egg compartments for mixing.

Step 5. Paint the inside of the egg carton. Add a bit of orange on the divider for the beak.

Step 6. Dab glue onto the bottom of the egg carton pieces. Press the glue onto a piece of card stock paper.

Step 7. Glue one cotton ball in each "eye" compartment. Attach one googly eye to each cotton ball using glue.

Step 8. Cut a piece of red cardstock paper into an amoeba shape to make the turkey's waddle. Fold the end under and glue it under the head.

Step 9. Create the feathers. This is messy fun for your child! Dip a cotton ball into one of the paint pools (use the tempera that is left over from paining the egg carton). Press another cotton ball into the first one, sharing the paint.

Step 10. Glue the cotton balls onto the paper on the sides of the body. Repeat the painting and gluing process for as many feathers as your child wants to make.

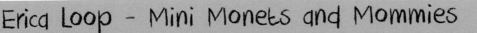

Erica Loop - Mini Monets and Mommies

MINI MONETS AND MOMMIES
Artsy Adventures for Moms (and Dads) and Kids

Erica Loop is a mom, blogger and arts educator. She has an MS in child development, and has been teaching children's art programs in museums and for community organizations for the past decade.
http://www.minimonetsandmommies.com/

Snowy Pinecone Owls

Fine Motor, Sensory, DIY Toys, Imagination Play

Pre-school

Kinder-garten

You will need:

One pine cone per child
Some cotton wool (we used about 1.5 "normal sized" bags)
Some felt in various colours (for eyes and beaks)
Googly eyes
A little glue at the very end

How to:

Step 1. Begin your activity by reading Owl Babies by Martin Waddell.
Step 2. Talk about shapes that you find on owls - circles for the eyes, triangles for the beak.
Step 3. Encourage the children to feel the prickly pine cones and the soft cotton wool. Wonderful contrasting for the senses... Then begin by "tearing" the cotton wool apart to make it smaller and stuff the pieces into the pine cones. No glue needed in this part of making your pine cone owl!
Step 4. Once your owl is "sufficiently stuffed", make sure there are no loose bits hanging out. Cut circle and and triangles for the children - if they are able and there is enough time, encourage the children to cut these themselves. Use a little white glue to stick these on. Once the felt and beak are in place, add googly eyes.

Maggy Woodley - Red Ted Art

Maggy Woodley, mum of 2, is passionate about crafts. You will find regular and great craft tutorials on her website Red Ted Art. She is also author of the equally named Red Ted Art book - packed with 60 fun crafts to do throughout the year. http://www.redtedart.com/

Felt Turkey Busy Bag

Fine Motor, Busy Bags, Color Learning, Shapes

Toddler

Pre-school

Kinder-garten

You will need:

Felt - brown, orange, yellow, red, blue, green and a background of your choosing
Googly eyes
Velcro
Scissors
Mod Podge or other fabric glue

How to:

I love busy bags. They are so wonderfully versatile and give you a screen-free option for when you need a quiet activity. And they're portable! One of my favorite ways to make a busy bag is by creating animal faces from felt pieces for my toddlers to put together. For Thanksgiving, we made a felt turkey busy bag. It was so easy and turned out to be really cute!

To make your own felt turkey, start by tracing a circle out of brown felt. This will be the body. I used a saucer and it was the perfect size. Cut out your circle.

Then cut out five teardrop shapes for feathers - red, blue, orange, yellow, & green. I did the first one freehand and then traced each subsequent one so they were fairly uniform.

Cut out a small diamond of yellow felt for the nose, a small teardrop shape out of red felt for the wattle, and two feet shapes out of orange felt.

Adhere a small square of Velcro to the back of two googly eyes. You want to put the stiffer hook side of the velcro on the back of

the eyes so that it will stick to the felt.

I actually experimented with two different sized eyes - I liked the bigger ones but my two-year-old thought it looked like an owl, so he chose a smaller size.

Next, cover the back of your brown felt circle in Mod Podge or fabric glue. Adhere this to the center of your background piece of felt. Allow to dry.

You now have all the pieces to make your turkey! I gave the turkey to one of my toddlers already assembled so he knew what it should look like. He immediately took all the pieces off and began trying to make his own turkey.

My toddlers love taking the turkey apart and putting it back together again. This is a great activity to put in a busy bag for restaurants, waiting rooms, or of course, the Thanksgiving table! No mess and they can play over and over again, even after Thanksgiving has passed. Too cute and so fun!

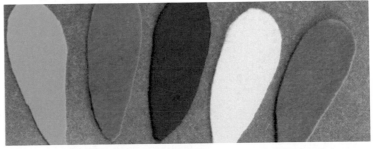

Laura R - Sunny Day Family

I'm Laura, a stay-at-home mom to twin toddler boys, two dogs and a cat. I love finding new ways to keep my family healthy and happy while trying to stay sane. You can find me at http://sunnydayfamily.com

Fine Motor Fall Yarn Wrapping

Fine Motor, Sensory

Toddler

Pre-school

Kinder-garten

You will need:

Yarn
Boxboard
Tape
Scissors

How to:

Making these beautiful yarn-wrapped fall shapes is a perfect way to spend a cozy autumn afternoon with your kids. They're fun for toddlers, preschoolers, older children, and even adults to make! The process is fantastic for developing fine motor skills, as those little hands will have to work to control the yarn and maneuver the wraps. Making them is also a great sensory experience--yarn is such a soft and pleasing material to work with! Here's how to make your own.

You'll need some yarn in fall colors. The type of fiber isn't important, but the nicer the yarn you use, the nicer they will feel to make.

Next, draw fall shapes on boxboard or thin cardboard. Leaves, apples, pumpkins, and acorns are all easy to draw. Cut out the shapes and then cut small notches all the way around the edges. The notches will give the yarn something to grab on to, especially around the curvier curves.

Secure the yarn to the back of your shapes with tape and then start wrapping! You can do them all willy-nilly crisscross, or line the wraps up in tidy rows. You can fully cover the shapes,

or leave lots of open space. When you're satisfied with how your shape looks, cut the yarn and tie the end to some of the wraps on the back of the cardboard.

Once you're done, these shapes could be added to a fall sensory bin, hung on a tree or a garland, or just set on a table to look pretty!

This basic craft technique can be adapted for so many different themes or topics. You can make basic geometric shapes, snowflakes, Christmas shapes or ornaments, flowers, Easter eggs, or even letters and numbers!

Ellen - Cutting Tiny Bites

Ellen is a former teacher who now channels all that energy into staying at home with her two young daughters. She writes at CuttingTinyBites.com about crafting, early learning, homeschool preschool, parenting ideas, and vegetarian cooking. http://www.cuttingtinybites.com/

Pumpkin Cloud Dough

Sensory, Play Recipes, Imagination Play

Pre-school

You will need:

4 cups of flour
1/2 cup of canola or vegetable oil
3 pieces of orange sidewalk chalk
Pumpkin Pie spice (found in the spice aisle at any local grocery store)

How to:

We LOVE sensory play activities at our house and we decided to celebrate fall by making some pumpkin-scented cloud dough.

If you've never heard of cloud dough, let me let you in on a little secret: It's amazing!
It's soft and powdery, but also squishy and moldable. And since it's so versatile, you can scoop it, pour it, sift it, shape it, mold it, and even use cookie cutters with it!
It's seriously so much fun that even I can't keep my hands out of it! Hey, moms need sensory play in their life, too!

Because sensory play is all about engaging the senses, what better way than to make something smell good? That's why we chose to scent our cloud dough with pumpkin! It smelled so good that we couldn't keep our noses out of it!

Crush your 3 pieces of orange sidewalk chalk by placing them in a baggie and just using a hammer to smash them. You want your chalk in powder form. If you don't have orange chalk, you can also use orange tempera powder paint.
In your designated sensory bin, pour the flour in and then add the oil. I find that the best ratio for the best cloud dough is 1/2 cup oil to every 4 cups of flour. Knead the flour and oil together.

After mixing the flour and oil, pour in your crushed sidewalk chalk to make your cloud dough orange. Once everything is mixed, add in the pumpkin pie spice until the flour is scented like pumpkin pie! There's no exact measurement, so just keep adding until the scent is just right for your kids.

Then it's time to PLAY! You can add whatever you'd like to your cloud dough. I like to give tools to scoop with such as an ice cream scoop or spoon, as well as cups, bowls, and shovels.

To enhance your pumpkin cloud dough experience even more, you could:
- add real pumpkin seeds to your play
- add real acorns to the bucket
- add some nutmeg or cinnamon for extra scent

I hope your little one loves playing with their pumpkin cloud dough!

Erica Leggiero - eLeMeNO-P Kids

ELEMENO-P KIDS
play. create. imagine.

Erica is a former preschool teacher with a M.Ed. in Elementary/Reading Education. She has taught children in some capacity since 2008. She firmly believes play is the way children learn. It is fun for them and they can learn about themselves, the people around them, their environments, and build skills needed for the big world! Erica is on a mission to inspire the mind, body, and spirit of your preschooler. http://www.elemenopkids.com/

Autumn/Fall Leaf Fairies

Fine Motor, Imagination Play, Color Learning, Counting, Size Sorting, Literacy

Toddler

Pre-school

Kinder-garten

You will need:

Some plain pencils or wooden sticks
Fine line permanent marker
Glue, sticky dots or sticky tape
Lots of different Fall leaves, all manner of colours, sizes and shapes

How to:

We took the plain pencils and with the fine line permanent marker, Peakles drew a simple face about an inch down from the top. We then counted out the leaves and ordered them by size, colour and shape. We also worked out the minimum leaves that were needed to decorate each fairy.

We selected some dry (not dried-out) leaves from the pile that we had collected. After some experimentation we found that leaves with points would make wonderful hair or crowns. Using some glue dots, we stuck the crown to the pencil above the face. We then used a variety of leaves to create dresses, skirts, tops and trousers. Eventually we had some fully clothed Fall Leaf Fairies.

In our garden we have a memorial urn for our pets which has a variety of flowers and plants in it. During the cooler months this can look a bit unloved and forlorn. Peakles decided this was a perfect place to place the Fall Leaf Fairies.

Over the next few months we observed how the Fall Leaf Fairies changed from brightly coloured leaves to ragged and dull ones, and we talked about their feelings. Eventually the leaves had

been broken down by the weather until only the face remained, which made us feel a little sad.

This proved to be a great source of inspiration for Peakles, who was fascinated by how the Fairies changed as the season changed. She became aware that things change and sometimes cannot be fixed or mended. This led to some interesting talks about life and the world around us.

Peakles also continued to talk about the Fairies and would include them in drawings and made up a whole story about where they might have flown to and why.

Helen - Peakle Pie

Helen is a former primary school teacher and art historian. She writes at Peakle Pie about all the creative and imaginative ideas that she explores with her daughter Peakles. They both love playing and learning at the same time. Since Peakles started school in September, Helen has been keen to balance her school time with play sessions that allow Peakles to explore, learn and just have fun. http://peaklepie.com/

Make Santa's Mailbox

Fine Motor, Imagination Play

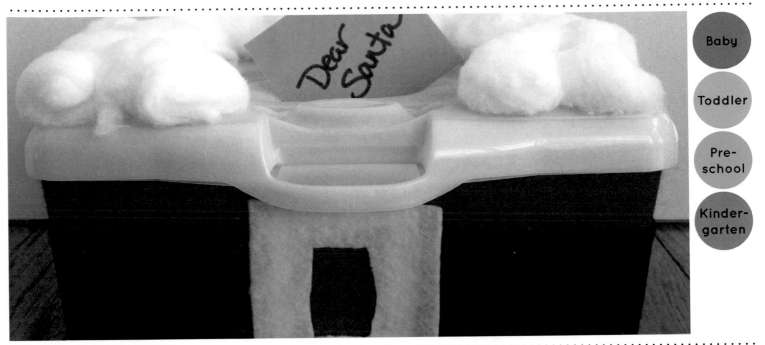

Baby

Toddler

Pre-school

Kinder-garten

you will need:

Baby wipes container or tissue box
Felt - red, black, yellow
Cotton balls
Scissors
Fabric glue

How to:

Santa's Mailbox is an easy Christmas craft that can be used to hold letters to Santa, or as a fun activity for toddlers who love to put things into boxes. Plus, it's frugal because it recycles an empty baby wipes container. If you don't have one you can still make this out of an old tissue box, but it won't be as sturdy.

To make your mailbox, first measure and cut your felt pieces. These were the sizes for my box, however depending on the brand you use you may need to adjust slightly:

Red – 4 inches wide by 23 inches long
Black – 1.5 inches wide by 11.5 inches long (2 of these)
Yellow – 2.5 inches square with a 1 inch x 1.5 inch rectangle, cut from the center

Coat the sides of your container with glue.

Wrap your red felt around the bottom of the container and pull tightly. You may need to apply a little more glue at the seam. Carefully trim any excess from the bottom so that it will sit evenly.

Allow to dry. Then put a very light coating of glue on the back of your two black rectangles. Wrap these around the center of your container, leaving a space in the front center for your belt buckle.

Apply glue to the back of the yellow piece and adhere to space in the front center of your container, connecting the 2 black pieces.

Coat the top of your container with glue, leaving the opening clear, and apply cotton balls. Press gently to make sure they stick.

Allow to dry, and Santa's ready for mail!

Santa's mailbox is the perfect spot for your kids to drop off their Christmas lists. It can also become an activity for toddlers to put cards into the box, then open it and start all over again.

You can also find a good use for all those holiday catalogs that come in the mail. They make great cutting practice for your little ones to cut out pictures and drop them into Santa's mailbox. You can also make "cookies" out of felt or construction paper and "feed" them to Santa.

Laura R - Sunny Day Family

I'm Laura, a stay-at-home mom to twin toddler boys, two dogs and a cat. I love finding new ways to keep my family healthy and happy while trying to stay sane. You can get to know me at http://sunnydayfamily.com.

Christmas Tree Race

Gross Motor, Color Learning, Shapes

Toddler

Pre-school

Kinder-garten

You will need:

Green construction paper or card stock
Scrap bits of paper in various colors
Scissors and/or craft punches
Laminator or clear sticky-backed plastic
Sticky tape

How to:

This Christmas Tree Race for toddlers and preschoolers is a fun and fast-paced learning game. We've used it for helping our children learn their shapes and colors. It can also be adapted for primary-aged kids for other subjects.

How to set up the Christmas Tree Race:
Simply cut a Christmas tree shape for each child from a piece of green construction paper and laminate them. Cut or punch various shapes from your paper scraps. Laminate and cut out the little shape "decorations."

Use some sticky tape rolled back on itself to hold the trees up on the window (thus they double as window decorations when not in use). However, I wouldn't advise having them on a window for the game itself. When you are ready to play, move the tree to a wall.

Place a bit of sticky-tape or rolled-up tape on the backs of the "decorations." Line them up on the floor on the other side of the room from the tree.

How to play the Christmas Tree Race:
Have the children stand behind the decorations and call out either a color or shape. The children then race to pick up the correct item and run to put it on their tree.
The first child to get their item on the tree wins that round. You can continue until one child has reached a pre-determined score, or until all of the decorations have been used.

This game will grow with your children as you can write numbers, letters, or words on the decorations. And when they're a bit older yet, they could pick up the answer to math questions: 10-4 =6 for example.

If you have only one child, you can race against them yourself or use a timer to see how full they can make the tree before their time is up.

This is also a great game to play to learn vocabulary in a second language! My children love this game as much as the students I taught in Japan did. And they still play it after three years. That's a keeper in my books.

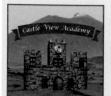

Crystal McClean - Castle View Academy

Crystal is an ex-pat home educating Mama who is passionate about her children, learning, crafting and frugality.
http://www.castleviewacademy.com/

Photo & Handprint Keepsake

Fine Motor, Sensory

Baby

Toddler

Pre-school

Kinder-garten

You will need:

Salt
Flour
Water
Photos
String

How to:

Last year I wanted to add a photo to our Christmas tree ornaments AND a keepsake too, so I combined the two: making a handprint AND photo keepsake ornament!

We used salt dough to make these pretty handprint photo keepsake:
1 cup of salt
1 cup of all purpose flour
1/4 to 1/2 cup of water
Mix until not sticky any more.

We added some red glitter to the dough, although we could have added more.

We then did the following:
- Rolled the dough out and pressed hands
- Cut around the handprint in a mitten shape
- Used a star shaped cookie cutter to make place for the photo "frame"
- Added the names and dates by using a bamboo stick and made a hole for the ribbon

It baked for about 3 hours, 100'C.
I added the photo at the back, and pulled a ribbon through, and voila! A cute keepsake ornament! We will be hanging ours on the tree, but it will look equally pretty on the wall after the Christmas season ends!

Nadia - Teach me Mommy

Nadia is a former preschool teacher, and currently works as a remedial therapist with elementary students. She is a mommy to 2 blessings and blogs at Teach me Mommy about easy and playful activities with the aim to teach, and the occasional DIY project. http://teach-me-mommy.com/

165

Cinnamon Gingerbread Man Craft

Fine Motor, Sensory

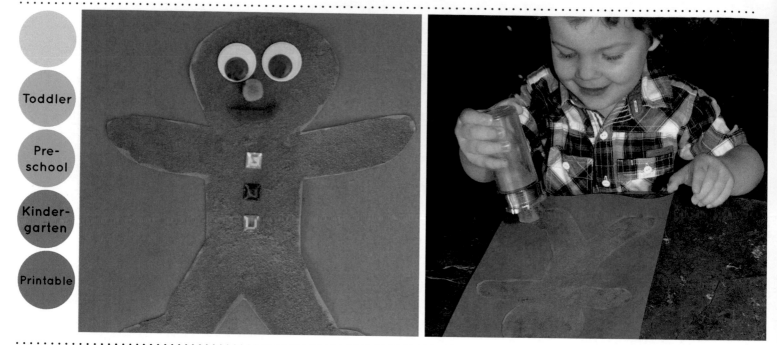

Toddler

Pre-school

Kinder-garten

Printable

You will need:

Brown construction paper
Construction paper for background of a different color (if desired)
Cinnamon in a shaker
Googly eyes
Scissors
Small pink pom pom, bead, or paper circle cut out for the nose
White glue
Glue stick (if desired or you can use white glue)
Plastic gems, beads, buttons, pom poms or anything else you like for the buttons
Red or pink felt or paper for mouth
Gingerbread man printable template

How to:

This craft is equally fun for toddlers, preschoolers and kindergarteners. You can vary how much you help them with the steps based on their age. Cut the brown construction paper down to the size of your printer paper. Download and print the gingerbread man template directly onto the brown paper. Cut it out for toddlers. Older children can practice their cutting skills by cutting out their own.

Have your child use the glue stick or white glue on one side of the gingerbread man and stick it to the background paper. You could glue it onto the background later, but the gingerbread man has a tendency to curl upward once it dries if it is not glued down, which makes it a little trickier to glue it to the background.

Have your child smell the cinnamon while it is still in the shaker. If you have other spices handy, have your children compare the scents. You can make a game of it by having them guess which one is the cinnamon out of a few choices with their eyes closed. You could make it easier by using very different scents such as oregano and sage or more challenging by using similar spices such as nutmeg and allspice.

Cut out a mouth from felt or paper. I think it is easier to make a mouth by folding the paper or felt in half first. If you are having the children cut it out, you may want to draw an outline onto the folded paper or fabric to make it easier for them.

Spread white glue all over the gingerbread man using fingers or a paintbrush. Have your child sprinkle cinnamon all over the gingerbread man and shake off the excess onto a piece of paper. You can save the excess in a bag if desired to use for future crafts (as long as it is not stored with the cinnamon used for cooking). Then, use the white glue to attach the gingerbread man's features.

Allow to dry.

Multiples = Multiple Blessings

Theresa - Capri + 3

Capri + 3 is full of arts and crafts, play, science and literacy activities for children. Theresa, a psychologist, now home with her four same-age preschoolers also shares family adventures, recipes and stories of parenting multiples. http://www.multiples-mom.com/

Hot Chocolate Taste Experiment

Sensory, Science Experiments, Kids In The Kitchen

Pre-school

Kinder-garten

Printable

You will need:

4 small mugs or cups per child
Hot chocolate printable
Small piece of peppermint candy
Cinnamon
Vanilla
Orange zest
Optional: small removable stickers

How to:

Engaging children's senses is one of the easiest and most effective ways to nurture brain development.

The more we engage children's senses, the more their brain has opportunities to make connections about the world around them, and build new understandings and structures, which help lay a good foundation for later learning.

It's usually pretty easy to figure out how to engage most of the senses, but the sense of taste can be a bit tricky – especially if you have picky eaters!

This hot chocolate tasting experiment isolates the sense of taste, while being inviting and exciting for the children. This is a great activity to encourage taste distinctions, and possibly widen your child's palate, as well as a great vocabulary builder!
For this introductory experiment, I went with festive holiday flavours, but you could alternatively select flavours that would engage each of the five taste categories – sweet, salty, bitter,

sour, and umami. (For those, I would suggest sugar, salt, small amount of coffee, small amount of orange or lemon juice, and soy sauce or tamari.)
Place a small amount of each flavour in separate mugs, then top with hot chocolate. Place the unused portions of the flavourings on a tray or plate for the kids to explore and compare to what they are tasting.

If using the stickers, add a sticker to the bottom of each mug to keep track of which mugs hold which flavours.

Then, serve the hot chocolate! Try to have the children guess which flavour is in each mug, and ask them to describe what they are tasting. Suggest descriptive words, and explain any new words to them.

After this activity, you could try offering "matching" mugs and having the children try to compare. You can also do seasonal variations of this – flavouring lemonade or even water!

Jennifer Tammy - Study at Home Mama

Jennifer Tammy is a Canadian Psychologist currently at home with her daughter, running a full-time Montessori daycare. She loves sharing parenting inspiration and hands-on learning ideas on her blogs!
http://studyathomemama.ca/

Emo Santa

DIY Toys, Imagination Play

You will need:

Cardboard tubes of differing diameters
Thin permanent marker
Acrylic paint
Felt
Pom pom
Hot glue gun

How to:

Make an Emo Santa toy! His facial expression changes, helping kids develop emotional intelligence and empathy through play.

To make one, you'll need to find two cardboard tubes that fit neatly inside one another. I've used the cardboard tube from plastic wrap (cling film) that has been trimmed to the height of the outer tube, and a toilet paper roll.

Cut a face-shaped hole in the outer tube, and then use this hole to measure where to draw the facial expression on the inner tube. Once you've drawn the first expression, twist the inner tube around until you see a blank space, and draw a contrasting expression. However, don't limit yourself to just happy and sad. What about worried, surprised, thoughtful, delighted? If you flip the inner tube upside down, you'll find space for more expressions.

I ended up making several of these inner tubes, so we now have over 20 facial expressions that my girls can choose from when they play.

Now that you have your facial expressions completed, put the inner tube aside, because it's time to turn the outer tube into a set of clothes!

I made the hat from red felt, a pom pom and a hot glue gun – which is also how I attached it to the top of the roll. Then I painted the edge of the hat, the hair and the beard using white acrylic paint, and the Santa suit using red, black and yellow acrylic paint.

Once he's dry, pop the inner tube back inside, and he's ready to play.

Toddlers will probably need you to choose the facial expression for them, and may not understand the subtleties between some of the facial expressions. By preschool age, most kids will be able to twist and turn the inner tube around to choose which facial expressions they want their character to be feeling.

You can make several outfits to encourage roleplay. We have this Santa outfit, Frosty, a mean 'Jack Frost,' two girls and a smaller fairy.

We made these dolls about 15 months or so ago, and they are still played with today. Somehow the sturdy inner tube protects the outer tube from being crumpled, so they have held up really well.

Which reminds me, I really should make a new outfit for the girls soon - an Emo Leprechaun perhaps?

Danya - Danya Banya

Danya is a fun Australian mum to two little girls. She's given up the corporate life to spend her days finger painting, making play dough and creating with toilet paper rolls. She shares ways to play and create with kids on her blog Danya Banya. http://www.danyabanya.com/

Fine Motor Button Tree

Fine Motor, Busy Bags

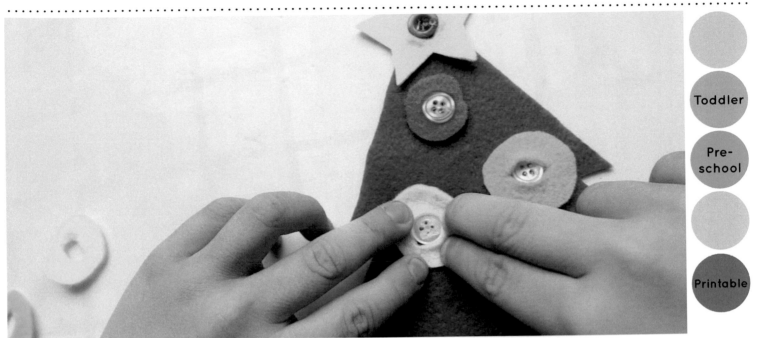

Toddler

Pre-school

Printable

You will need:

Various colors of felt
Buttons
Hot glue gun

How to:

This Christmas Busy bag has a heavy focus on fine motor skills by using buttons.

To make this busy bag cut out a tree in green felt (see the template) then make dots with hot glue on the tree felt and stick down the buttons. YES! that's right! NO SEWING!

Next cut a few colorful felt circles and make small slits about the length of the buttons in the middle. You can use a spare button to measure this before you cut.

Make sure you also cut a star for the top! (Use the template star if you are unable to free hand cut).

Have fun using your new busy bag and decorating that tree!!

Nicolette Roux - Powerful Mothering

Hi I'm Nicolette, a SAHM to 4 little ones age 5 and under. I love to share my simple and easy crafts & activities, printables and learning ideas for 0-5 year olds! Author of: Rice Play and 99 Fine Motor ideas for Ages 1-5.
http://www.powerfulmothering.com/

Christmas Egg Drop Project

Fine Motor, Math, Science, Science Experiments

Pre-school

Kinder-garten

You will need:

Christmas Straws
Tissue Paper
Wrapping Paper Scraps
Bows
Ribbon
Eggnog Containers
Garland
Tinsel
Eggs
Christmas Washi Tape
Scissors

How to:

With all the materials set out in an inviting format, the boys were ready to dig in. What I love most about Egg Drop Projects, is the flexibility and creativity it allows.

There is no RIGHT WAY to the EGG DROP! If there were, would I ever have designed something like my son? No way! Would your child design something like this? That is the fun of the project and the science behind it. Allow your children to predict, test, and modify their projects until they find a design that works for them.

Challenge your children to create a structure for a raw egg, that protects the egg from cracking at any height of a fall. After your children have built the perfect contraption, have them place their egg on the inside and get ready for the real test.

Find the perfect place to "test" your contraption. We used the front stairs, the neighbor's porch and our second story window but you can try a variety of places. You can add in math by measuring the height or timing the falls.

Finally, check your egg. Did it survive? Did it crack? Failures are just as important as the successes. They allow us to reevaluate, assess what works, and what doesn't and teaches us to be resilient.

Dayna Abraham - Lemon Lime Adventures

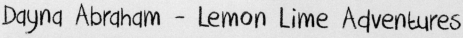

Dayna is a National Board Certified teacher with over 12 years of experience in the primary classroom. She recently began homeschooling her 3 children against her will. She writes at Lemon Lime Adventures, where she writes about the trials, successes and errors of their life, life living as a blended family, and dealing with a son with Sensory Processing Disorder. http://www.lemonlimeadventures.com/

DIY Animal Party Blower Craft

DIY Toys, Imagination Play, Color Learning

Toddler

Pre-school

Kinder-garten

You will need:

Paper plate
Paint
Pom poms
Straw
2 inch x 6 inch paper
Scotch Tape
Tissue Paper

How to:

With the new year just around the corner, I've been looking for fun, festive crafts and activities for toddlers and preschoolers. I know the kids won't get to bed on time (and thus let mommy and daddy ring in the New Year) unless there are some super creative activities to help them celebrate early and burn off energy.

What better way to release that energy than to let the party animal in them out for some fun!

I started working on a quick DIY party blower idea and then adapted it to a party animal craft I found from Kix.com to complete my DIY New Year's craft (which can also be used for birthday parties)!

Let your kid paint one side of the paper plate red or a pinkish color (for the party animal's mouth). Set aside to dry for an hour or two and gather materials to create the blower piece.

Cut up some left over wrapping paper approximately 2-inches by 6-inches. Fold the sides over so that they meet in the center to create a seam. Secure with scotch tape. Now looking at the paper length-wise, fold one end in about 1/4 of an inch and secure with tape. Next, curl the paper in. (You can use a pencil or straw to curl in easier and temporarily clip it so it remains curled after blowing.)

Attach the other end to a straw and secure with tape. You can use a full-size straw or cut in half for a better fit. Add some tissue paper to create a more festive look with fringe!

Have your kid paint the other side of the plate another bright color. Once dry, use a hot glue gun to attach the pom pom eyes to the top of the plate. Make sure the eyes are at a 90 degree angle so they look straight out.

Poke a hole in the center of the plate to insert the blower and complete the craft!

This is a great New Year's craft to make with kids of all ages and can also be used to celebrate birthdays and other parties throughout the year!

Ana Taney - Mommy's Bundle

I'm Ana, a mom to two lovable little boys: one baby and one toddler. At MommysBundle.com I share my parenting insight for new moms seeking support for everything from pregnancy prep and baby care to managing life with a rambunctious toddler. I often share my must-have parenting tips, favorite products and activities to keep the little ones entertained as they grow. http://mommysbundle.com/

Index

Clothesline Matching

Print the clothes and hang them on the line

Therapy Fun Zone

Clothesline Matching
Print the clothes and hang them on the line

Therapy Fun Zone

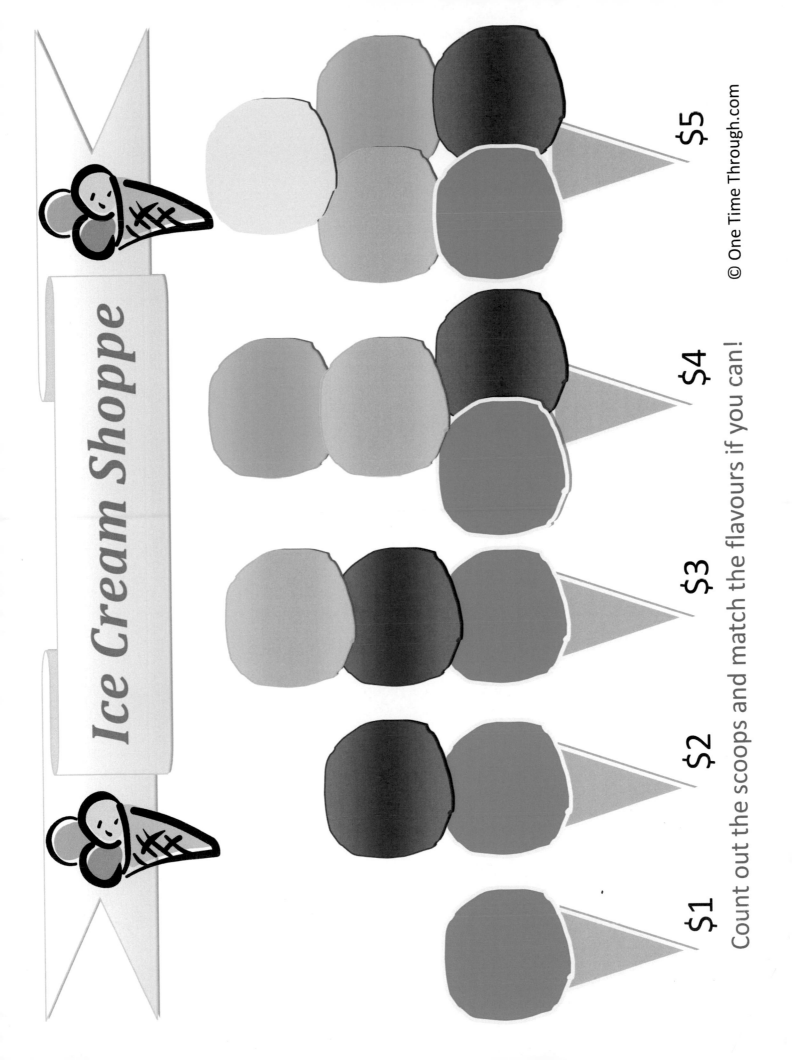

Ice Cream Shoppe

$5

$4

$3

$2

$1

Count out the scoops and match the flavours if you can!

STORY WRITING PROMPT

People
Mum
Me
Lily
Zach
Mae
Daddy
Doodles

Beginning
Once upon a time...

There was a boy/girl called...

One night Millie was...

This story is about...

One day I ...

Places
At home
Seaside
Garden
Shops
Work
Playground
Zoo

Middle

"person" went to "place"
When they got there "this" happened
They did..."something"
It was...
They were with...
They were happy/sad...

End
Finally "this" happened
Then they went to...
Everyone was happy
They all lived happily ever after
...went to bed
...went home

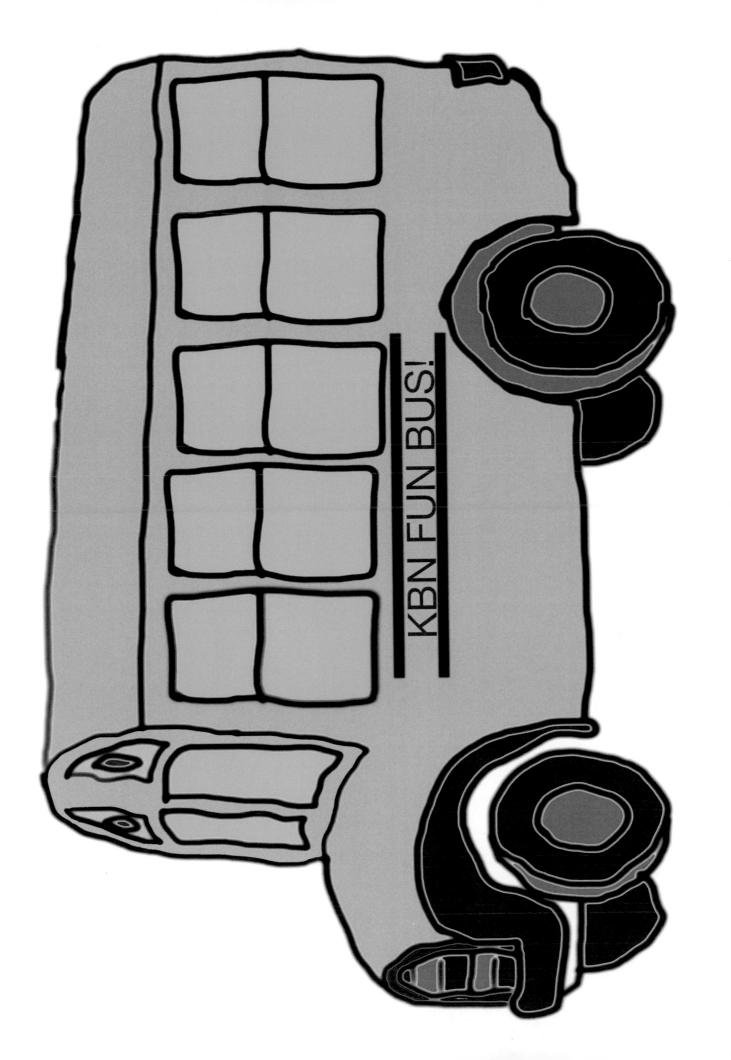

	red	yellow	blue	orange	green	purple
10						
9						
8						
7						
6						
5						
4						
3						
2						
1						

Morning Routine

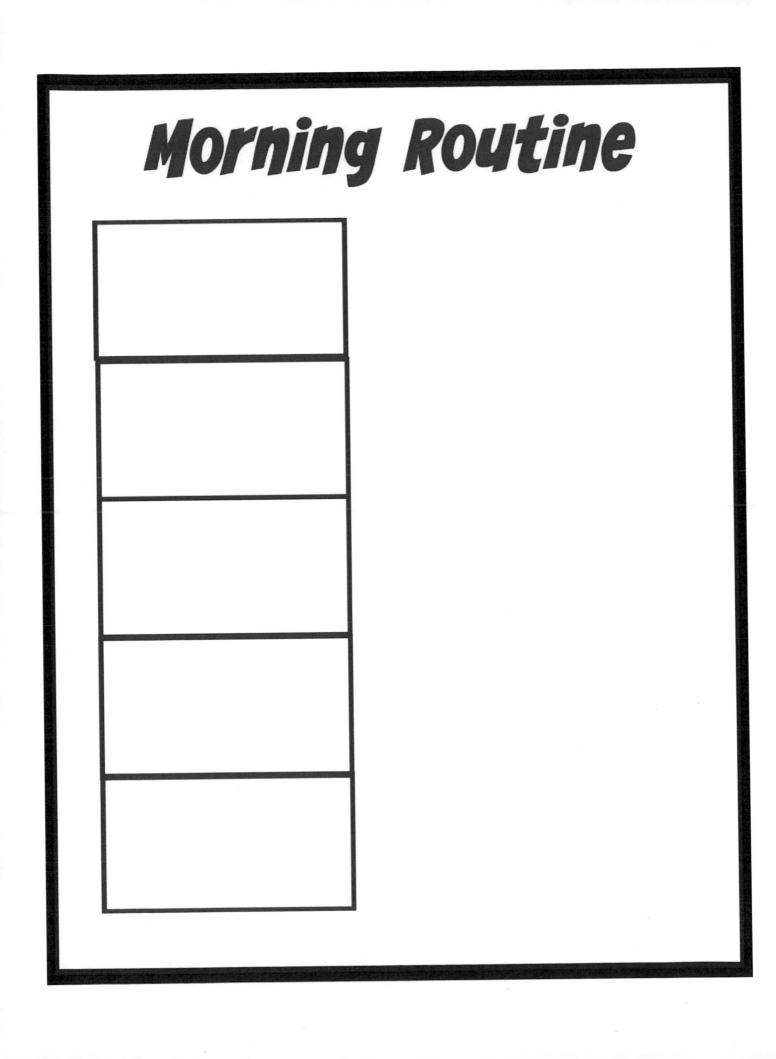

Night Routine

COUNT

DOWN

THE

DAYS

UNTIL

H
A
L
L
O
W
E
E
N

healthy hot chocolate

In a sauce pan combine and whisk

1 cup milk

1 tbsp honey

2 tbsp tbsp cocoa powder

1 tsp vanilla

Study at Home Mama

healthy hot chocolate

In a sauce pan combine and whisk

1 cup milk

1 tbsp honey

2 tbsp tbsp cocoa powder

1 tsp vanilla

Study at Home Mama

48214582R10113